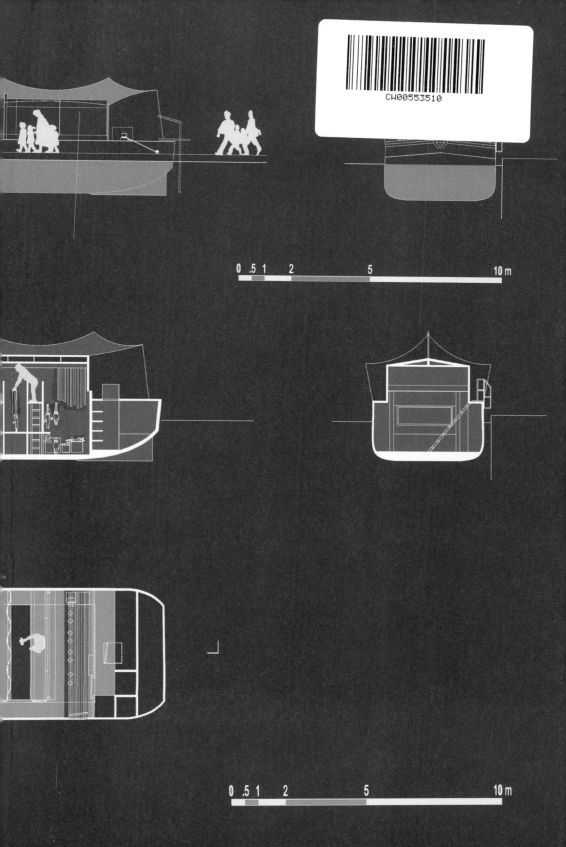

0 .5 1   2   5   10 m

0 .5 1   2   5   10 m

Keeping Afloat

An adventure
on a river barge that became a theatre

Middleton & Rogers

Dedication

This book is dedicated to
Natasha, Katherine, Louise, Rob and
Stanley, Joshua and Thomas.

© Grenville Middleton, 2019

Published by Mule Publishing

A CIP catalogue record for this book is available from the British Library.

ISBN 978-0-9931700-1-0

Book layout and jacket design by Clare Brayshaw

Prepared and printed by:

York Publishing Services Ltd
64 Hallfield Road
Layerthorpe
York
YO31 7ZQ
Tel: 01904 431213

Website: www.yps-publishing.co.uk

Preface

Sometime ago we attended a performance of a production performed by a Georgian company under the direction of Rezo Gabriadze, a man who had been brought up when his country was part of the Russian empire. In the programme he stated "I am possessed by a deep desire for freedom. Something pushes me to pursue it." With that thinking it is no wonder that he turned to puppetry, for it is the art of puppetry that offers the artist the freedom to explore writing, painting, sculpting, acting and design.

And so, here we have attempted to explain what drove us to create a theatre, where we could find that freedom to present our shows as we wished, without compromise. The fact that it happened to be on a barge is purely because nowhere could we find a land-based venue within our means. But, as it turned out, this was the best way fate could have led us, as a travelling theatre, especially on water, is a positive advantage. Everything moves as one, staging, seating, puppets and puppeteers.

Both of us had other trainings and careers before joining forces in the puppet world. This gave us valuable experience and maturity to draw on, but nothing could have prepared us for the adventures, frustrations and crises that lay ahead especially in the early years. Fortunately we had a dream, and alongside of it a good deal of energy, naivety, recklessness and determination. This, and the unfailing support of our family, friends and puppeteers made it possible for the dream to come true.

Gren Middleton
Juliet Rogers
London
5 May 2018

Acknowledgements

We would like to thank Jane Perrott, who originally recorded an oral history of the Puppet Barge, giving us much to draw on when memory failed; Sarah Fitzpatrick for typing it; Judy Cato for supplying photos of Richmond; Russel Debnam for apprenticeship details during the barge conversion; Arijit Chatterjee and Asha Sumra for the accurate scale drawings of the barge; Kate, Rob, Natasha and Louise for their support and for supplying dates and correcting details; Wendy Cope for her generous foreword; David Mercer and Clare Brayshaw, the team at York Publishing Services for design and managment; and finally, but most importantly, our gratitude goes to Sam Cook for her wonderful, encouraging and good humoured editing. Thank you all.

Contents

Foreword

This is the story of two people who have devoted their lives to their art: the art of marionette theatre. Although I know Gren and Juliet and have had the privilege of working with them, I have learned a great deal about them and their endeavours from this account. I've made several visits to their enchanting theatre barge without appreciating the effort involved in finding the right vessel, converting it and managing to get it to the place where they wanted to moor it (which involved some hair-raising moments).

I knew about their travels around England, putting on performances in Henley, Marlow and Abingdon, as well as in Little Venice and Richmond. But I had no idea they had taken their productions (minus barge) to Pakistan and Palestine.

The range of Movingstage productions is impressive. Gren and Juliet have no truck with the idea that puppet theatre is just for kids. They have staged works by Coleridge and Lorca and more than one Shakespeare play, as well as tales such as Red Riding Hood, which are suitable for the very young. I am especially grateful to them for their interest in commissioning work from living authors, such as Howard Barker and myself. Their interpretation of my narrative poem, The River Girl, has delighted me every time I've seen it.

Why do they do it? Here's a revealing quotation from the book. "Certainly, it wasn't fame that we were after, or riches" What motivated them, they go on to say, was "an inner drive to create and present marionette theatre." The words of true artists.

Wendy Cope
August 2018

List of Donors

The following people and organizations contributed to the construction and creation of the Puppet Theatre Barge that opened in January 1982.

Mrs Ruth Atkin

Mr Leon Blackman

Mr Peter Buckingham

Mr Edward Burd

Ms Rosemary Davies

Mr Ben Derbyshire

Mr Paul Deverall

Ms Geraldine Easter

The English Tourist Board

Mr and Mrs David and Jill Goldkorn

Ms Dana Norgren

Hackney Youth Workforce

Mrs Suze Hails

Ms Anna Hegarty

Hunt Thompson Associates

Mt Lawrence Isaacson

Mr Carrick James

London Weekend Television

Ms Jacqui Lyons

Mr Anthony McCloughlin

The Michael Marks Trust

Mrs Kathleen Middleton

Mr Nigel Morgan

Mr Eric Norgren

Redaluma Paint Company

Mr Chris Spencer

Thames Television

Mr John Thompson

Mr David Welsh

Mrs Anna Yallop

Chapter 1

Reasoning

... and all things be thought upon
That may, with reasonable swiftness, add
More feathers to our wings.
William Shakespeare
Henry V, Act 1, Scene 2

This is a history of a marionette theatre and of the family that created it and who are its proprietors. One might call us "marionette proprietors", and as such we will tell this story together. Marionette theatre is very special and rare. A marionette show can be seen as a psychological experience, an interaction contracted between the marionettist, a trained professional, and an audience. The difference between the actor's theatre and the puppet theatre is the presence of a doll that is "alive" and creates yet another channel of interaction with the audience.

We will start with Juliet, who, with her partner, Gren, was responsible for the creation of the Movingstage Marionette Company. Before the decision to form Movingstage came about they had been married for sixteen years. For nine of those years, during the 1970s, Juliet had been a trainee and an apprentice at the Little Angel Theatre in London. She started in the workshop, learning about making marionettes: carving, stringing and costuming. Then, about four years into her time at the company, she moved on to the performance side. She was often backstage when a show was being mounted, and one day, when one of the marionettists was not available, she was asked if she would like to fill the gap. Realising this was a really great aspect of the business, she accepted, promptly fell in love with the performance side of the art, and has been in love with it ever since. For the second half of that Little Angel period, Juliet was both making and performing, but probably more performing, and learning a lot about that. She also introduced our three daughters to the puppet theatre and they, after some early training at the Little Angel, went on to work with us.

A Hopi Kachina doll, the Mudhead Clown

Gren's introduction into marionette society was a fairly drawn-out process. In the 1970s, while Juliet was at the Little Angel, he worked in the film business as a freelance cameraman. After a seminal experience photographing a documentary that required him to live with the Hopi people in Arizona – the Hopi teach their children with the use of Kachina dolls, the embodiment of spirits that help or punish as necessary – he began to see the light, whatever that may be. Back home, without having previously given a moment's thought to the puppet business, he was drawn in to help at the Little Angel.

In 1976, John Wright, OBE, master marionettist at the Little Angel, invited Gren to join the company, primarily to drive his truck on a tour that would take the company through Europe to Greece for a festival of medieval and popular theatre. Both Juliet and the girls – twins Natasha and Katherine aged fourteen and Louise, eleven – were part of the company.

Gren thought that it would be a good idea to make a film about this tour, which involved taking a travelling theatre from England overland to Greece, through Germany and into Yugoslavia, which at that time was a communist country that was of interest to him. He then asked a director friend of his, Mike Pearce, who had worked with him on the Hopi production, if he would be interested in making such a film. Mike agreed and somehow, they got the equipment and film stock together and set off with John Wright and company.

Lyndie and John Wright

We had a wonderful tour that summer with the company, travelling through Germany and giving a couple of performances, which Mike and Gren filmed. In

The festival poster

addition to his camerawork and driving the truck, Gren also helped out with lighting for the puppet theatre.

We eventually arrived on the island of Zakynthos in Greece, where the Greeks welcomed us and made us feel at home. The festival was a well-funded, international affair. We witnessed various puppet performances and saw and met Dario Fo, the Italian writer, who was not famous at that time. It was fantastic to watch his mime performance.

There were some big companies from Poland, Bulgaria and Romania participating, and one from Russia as well. They were all very well funded by their communist governments, who saw puppet companies as useful on the propaganda side. Gren noticed that they had lovely big coaches to carry equipment and a large number of technicians. In fact, they had everything that our film business had and that our puppet companies didn't! As the adventure progressed it slowly dawned on Gren that the

marionette theatre was a really interesting medium, and by the end of the tour he was hooked. He now felt that the puppet business might well be an art form that he would be interested in. He also met George Speaight at the festival, the author of a seminal history on the English puppet theatre; they later became friends and worked together with a set of historical puppets, the Tiller-Clowes marionettes, which are now in the Victoria and Albert Museum.

George Speaight and Gren with two Tiller puppets, performing at the Museum of London in the 1980s

From that time on, Gren, who had become aware of the creative limitations that the film industry imposed on him, grew increasingly interested in the puppet theatre and began to watch and learn. Back in London he helped with the lighting at the Little Angel Theatre quite regularly. Finally, he joined the company on a couple of tours, sometimes swapping places with Juliet so that one parent could stay at home and take care of our family of teenage girls.

At this stage neither of us was aware of the metamorphosis that was taking place nor what lay ahead and how our lives would be changed.

Chapter 2

The Beginning

All you need in life is ignorance and confidence; then success is sure.

Mark Twain

(December 2, 1887)

Having had a good time touring and now slowly getting back to the reality of life in London, we decided that there was a future in the puppet business and Gren began to look into it as deeply as possible. At that point he had been in the TV and film industry for about twenty years, having photographed a few feature films and a number of documentaries. He was fairly successful but decided that he wasn't doing enough creative work. He explains: "I thought I was more like a toolmaker or a bricklayer, having perfected a craft while the others, whoever they might be, were doing the really creative work. In the film business, in the first instance you have the writer, who does the original work. The producer has a chance in as much as he or she gets a whole team together and can see the end project. So, the producer chooses the director, the writer, the cameraman, all the stars, the actors and so on. The director muscles in on the act and tries to get as much as can be had, although the position is really just that of an organiser. After that you have the editor, the composer, the designer, who all take as much as they can grab. Finally, you get to the lighting cameraman who thinks there is a lot of creative work – but theirs is the work of a glorified technician, a craftsman who knows how to light a scene, working to a formula.

The script tells you what the lighting should be and then you just interpret that; you don't actually invent the scene. That had become clear to me by then. So, I was looking for an outlet where I could express myself. Suddenly puppetry was offered to me, by luck and the wisdom of a cool partner who had extensive knowledge encompassing shadow puppets, string puppets, puppets big and small, presented in many different media from cabaret to film, theatre to street performance, and so on.

Deciding we would have to hone ourselves down to one speciality we chose marionettes (string puppets). Not many people use them and Gren, being quite an ambitious person, thought that with scant competition he could get to the top of the trade quite quickly. Little did he know that the reason for the lack of competition was that the marionette is notoriously difficult to make and present. He had a partner who knew the business. Ho ho.

There is a great advantage in being interested in the same work and art as your partner. You can discuss things for hours at various points in the day and night – during meals, in bed, while shopping or travelling and at all sorts of other times – which is what we did. We decided we would set up our own show and company. Both of us had learned a lot from John Wright during our time at Little Angel. In effect Gren had two years of a traineeship and Juliet many more, so together we took our turn, and, at the end of 1978, we set up our own company.

Fortunately for us, we already had a house in Islington for which we'd paid £3800; a significant piece of history, given the rise in

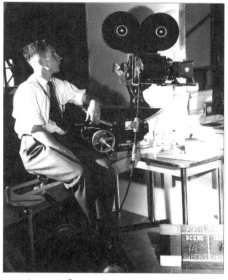

A greenhorn apprentice posing; Gren c. 1956

property values. We managed to sell it for £30,000 and bought a house in Hackney for £19,000. After all expenses we ended up with £10,000 in cash under the bath, so to speak. And that financed the puppet company. We bought a trailer and lighting equipment and built a stage.

As well as our puppetry training, we had other qualities. Having been brought up in the colonies, where you have to learn how to make things work, because there's no one to call on to help, Gren had good practical skills. He knew how to keep a van going, and with his knowledge of

Middleton Lodge; our home and workshop

lighting and electricity we had real help in getting started. A friend once said, "I can fix anything that works" and basically that was our position. Juliet, meanwhile, was an avid reader, a person who always had a book in her hand, so her knowledge of literature was a huge asset.

Coincidentally, at the time when we were trying to decide what was to be our first presentation, Mike Shrigley, an old friend of Juliet's, was visiting. He was a lecturer in English at Uppsala University, in Sweden, and happened to have with him a translation of the narrative poem *Sir Gawain and the Green Knight*. This unique piece of writing was the first published poem in the English language, c. 1400. The original is preserved in the British Museum.

The translation from Middle English was by Brian Stone, professor of English literature at the Open University. After reading it we both agreed to go ahead and make a production of the story. Gren wrote to Professor Stone and asked him if we could use his translation and he replied saying that he was very pleased to allow this.

We made the show and we still present it now, more than thirty years on, and it still sells out. For some reason it is amazingly popular. It was made primarily for adults, but it has such a wide universal appeal – good triumphing over evil; magic, mystery and adventure – that children can enjoy it too. Maybe it is true that once a child reaches the age of eight he/she is, practically speaking, grown-up. Is it the Jesuits who say, "give me the child for the first seven years and I will give you the man"? With our grandchildren, we had a chance to have a little influence on their upbringing between the ages of one and eight, but after that each became their own boss.

We try not to be ageist, but nowadays, of course, the publications that list performances always want to define the show in some kind of category, usually by age. A piece like *Sir Gawain and the Green Knight* is, we think, suitable for anyone who wants to watch it. Everyone, of whatever age, takes what they can out of it.

In order to present *Sir Gawain*, we built a portable marionette stage for long-string marionettes. This involves the puppeteer standing on a bridge and operating the puppet on the stage below so that the audience cannot see the operator but is able to see right through to a backcloth. There is not a puppeteer in sight, so no comparison in size is made and a greater illusion becomes possible. This form of staging allows for immense depth and perspective. We carried sophisticated lighting, controlling it from the bridge where we could literally paint with light while the show was going on.

This process was semi-pioneering, following in the footsteps of John Wright and others who had been presenting drama with marionettes quite regularly over the years. Marionette theatre became very fashionable in the eighteenth century, after Martin Powell arrived from Dublin. Powell opened a puppet theatre in St Martin's Lane. At one time there were seventeen marionette theatres in the West End: in the early nineteenth century, one such was owned by Charlotte Charke the daughter of a poet laureate. Although there are very few people presenting marionette drama today – you could probably count them on one hand – we were following a tradition.

Whenever possible we would take the show out as a family, all three girls having become proficient operators and performers following their experiences at Little Angel. One memorable date was the Festival of Fools in Penzance, Cornwall, in the summer of 1979. We camped on-site with other companies and gave several performances. This was our first meeting with Footsbarn Theatre company, who we met again on several occasions at the Albion Fairs in Suffolk. We were always inspired by their work. They presented a wonderful mix of magic and good writing with original and exciting stagecraft. During one of their productions they filled a huge tent with theatrical fog, through which appeared a gleaming sword, Excalibur.

Foreground: Juliet. Back row left to right: Natasha, Louise, Katherine, Gren

We soon discovered that when you want to tour you need funding. As a result, you come across the Arts Council or the British Council, both of which are managed by very well-educated Oxbridge types. You soon realise that if you are going to have any success in receiving funding you have to learn to speak the same language as the people who are giving the funds. So, it is quite difficult for ordinary people to muscle in on the act. The secret is to hire someone who speaks this language, but that was out of the question in the early days. We had to take on jobs without any funding, writing to venues, asking them to employ us. It wasn't long before Gren realised that he did not want to write for a job every two minutes.

We worked out that we had to get to the source. We needed a theatre of our own and, not only that, one specifically for marionettes. The writer, Jean Genet, once suggested to an Italian architect, who was about to build an arts centre incorporating a theatre with all the flexibility in the world, that he should withdraw all his plans immediately. The theatre should be fixed and inflexible. It should perhaps be built in a cemetery; imagine a performance of *Don Giovanni* in such a venue, he added. With this story in mind we deduced that if we were going to produce marionette theatre we would have to have a dedicated space for the art. If we were to present this art form to the public, we needed every aspect of our presentation to be in harmony.

We weren't alone in feeling this way. Puppet master and performer Barry Smith, who had been a voice coach to Laurence Olivier when he acted the part of Othello for the National Theatre, toured his own shows – including a memorable production of *Faustus* – using rod puppets. However, finding that venues and managements were not in sympathy with what he was presenting, he told us that he had become fed up with touring.

By now we had done a certain amount of land touring and decided we should listen to what the sages said and learn from them. Gren had realised that a marionette production is such a delicate balance between poetry, music and live theatre, and there is such competition from television and all other media entertainments, that we would have to get everything in order if our productions were to be seen as we wished them to be seen.

On one touring date we went to Crosby Civic Centre, a really nice music venue with the seating stretched out, fifty seats from one side to the other. Hopeless sight lines! What we needed was a venue with a maximum of ten seats across so that the audience could look straight down to the centre of our little stage, enjoying perfect sight lines.

The local authority officer who'd engaged us in Crosby had sold every seat, so there were approximately five hundred people watching a show presented by twenty-inch puppets! Audience members who sat at the back or the sides could not see anything. It was so awful and frustrating that we just had to think about creating our own venue. We were effectively driven to do it.

While working for John Wright we had noticed that on Friday afternoons, while the staff were enjoying a cup of tea and a bit of banter, he would be struggling with the payroll, VAT and various other matters. To run a fixed venue would require the same dedication to things that no artist could enjoy – and if they do enjoy them they are probably no artist.

It does not take much knowledge of maths or showmanship to realise that keeping a theatre open in one place requires an awesome number of productions. And marionette productions take a long time to make.

However, when you make your own shows, you are able decide what you want to present and what you want to say. You can, if you're subtle enough, infiltrate the show with your own politics, your own message. You have the chance to make a child aware of something so big and important that they carry the thought into adulthood. And if they become Prime Minister, they could change the whole structure of the country's laws! There is the chance. We are not saying that it happens, but at least you have that chance. Whereas if you're making films as a cameraman …?

If you present shows for people who are aged between three and eight and you present them well, with drama and strong content, they are likely to remember them for the rest of their lives. Even if they don't become Prime Minister, if you are presenting good stuff, they're going to be influenced in a good way and ultimately society is going to be improved. That was our theory.

While we were touring, a million and one influences affected us and one experience after the next started to make the two of us think. In our heads was the constant thought – "*We want a theatre – a small theatre!*" – and so, of course, we looked around. But by this point properties similar to the one John Wright had found for the Little Angel – a bombed-out temperance hall in a downtrodden, seedy area (which Islington was in those days) – were no longer available. John had managed to find a really good bargain, a theatre, a workshop and a cottage, all for around £4000, which even then was remarkable. By 1979 property values in London had already started to rise quite dramatically. We did find one old community hall in the far East End but realised that we were not going to get an audience for a marionette show down there. It was far too tough. They'd be more likely to come and bash you than come and see your show! So that was no good.

Then we began to think about trucks; could we make a theatre in a truck? Or a big tent? At that time there was a successful company called the Bubble Theatre that operated out of a tent. All these ideas were going through our heads when suddenly the notion of a boat presented itself. In *Time Out* magazine, Gren had seen a magic lantern show listed which was being given on a narrow boat. We decided to look for it and found the boat on a mooring at Little Venice. It was beautifully decorated with a built-in sixteen-seat theatre for presenting magic lantern slides.

Doug Lear, who ran the theatre with his wife Anita, was obsessed with slides and projectors built no later than 1920. He operated an old-fashioned magic lantern using painted glass slides and he had done the boat up very nicely. It was called *Phantasmagoria*. Doug struggled with British Waterways, which was not supportive; he was always having difficulties with his moorings and received no co-operation. Later, it seemed to us that the workers on the canal did not really like boats, so perhaps it wasn't Doug's fault, just how things were at the time.

The Lears toured their theatre until, following the birth of two babies, it became impossible for them to live on the boat and present shows there. It was quite a sad end. They went to Wales and we don't know whether they are still doing their shows. The fact of the matter was that the seeds of the theatre-on-a-boat idea had been planted in our heads and had germinated. The serious research began.

We had started the business at the end of 1978 and had given our first performance in March 1979 at the International Festival of Puppetry. By the end of 1980, Gren was busy dashing here and there and learning about the canal.

First he started looking at narrow boats, soon seeing that they were too narrow for a theatre, and realising that we needed a big, wider barge. The vision at this point was of touring romantically around the whole of Britain, France, Europe – even to the Black Sea and only heaven knows where else. Our imagination carried us forward. Running alongside that was the notion of simply travelling on the river. Gren saw a space, a space big enough for our proposed theatre. While looking for places where you could moor a boat and get an audience on and off safely, he found a hidden canal basin, virtually on our doorstep. Kingsland Basin, neglected and derelict, was just down the Kingsland Road, around the corner from us in Hackney.

It was amazing. There was nothing going on there, just this wonderful lost asset from a bygone age that no one had discovered. It had gone to pieces, basically. In 1948 the waterways had been nationalised to become British Waterways. We were looking at the basin thirty years later, by which time canals were no longer used for freight, and nationalised companies were seemingly falling into disrepute – probably owing to the effects detailed by Laurence J Peter in his book *The Peter Principle*. Canal workers liked manipulating the water but seemed to have no interest in boats. We guessed that the chairman of the board would have preferred to be chairman of British Rail but had never quite made it, and that the guy heading British Rail might have rather been the head of IBM and so on, all the way down to the leading canal man. They had all reached their level of incompetence and that was really the problem.

Gren had to do some research to find out more, so he found his way to the basin. On the one side there was a big cement works. He realised that it would be possible to see the basin from the cement works' yard. He went into the works and asked the foreman if he could go in and look at the basin. The man said he could. It was raining slightly, so the yard was covered with water. Gren cut across the yard underneath a conveyor belt and fell straight into a pit – a cement pit. He was sinking fast when a number of men ran out into the yard shouting. They managed to grab hold of him and pulled and pulled and got him out. He was entirely covered in wet cement. He thanked them, acting very cool, said he was sorry for the trouble caused and carried on. He went and looked at the canal; he was determined. He didn't realise that the cement was drying slowly. By the time he got home, about half to three-quarters of an hour later, the cement was hardening and burning his skin, so off came all his clothes as he jumped into a bath. He just lay there in the water getting all the lime off his burning body. The adventures one can have are quite unexpected.

That was just one adventure experienced while researching the canal. This was towards the end of 1980. Christmas came and went and 1981 presented itself with Margaret Thatcher in the driving seat. Watch out girls, boys and the rest!

Chapter 3

More Beginnings

Mind your head at all times.
Warning notice on the MV Maybrent

We were still searching for the right boat and the space to moor it – Kingsland Basin was too derelict to attract an audience – when Gren came across some barges in Islington's City Road Basin. He thought they looked promising as they were wide enough. He traced the owners and found that they belonged to Charrington's Coal & Coke Company, which said he could buy one for £3800.

This was a positive advance, and at this point we thought we should find a marine surveyor as our knowledge of boats was limited. We knew about houses to a certain extent, having had a fair amount of experience with renovations, but boats were another matter. Looking in the *Yellow Pages* we found a phone number for the Royal Institution of Naval Architects. An enquiry to them produced a lead to three marine surveyors.

The first person Gren spoke to said he used to survey Royal Navy battleships and wasn't interested in a canal barge, but he knew a certain Jack Hall who, he said, "… knows about that sort of thing, about those river boats, canal stuff – contact him".

He gave Gren a number. Excitement was building. Gren phoned Mr Hall and asked him if he would look at the barges. Jack Hall then asked how much Charrington wanted for one and when he was told about £3000, he replied, "… far too much, far too much, leave it with me". Gren agreed to do so, but both of us felt mildly disappointed as we were dying to get started. We had the three thousand ready, burning a hole in whatever pocket it was in.

And so we waited. A week went by, and Jack Hall didn't phone. We waited another week until, on the Saturday morning, Gren could not contain himself any longer and phoned Jack's number. His wife answered and said he was "down at the yard; give him a ring down there". She gave Gren the number of the yard; he phoned and asked for Mr Hall. After a moment a gruff voice answered, "Can you get down here now?" So Gren got in the car and drove like a demon through the Blackwall Tunnel, turned left and followed the road round. Eventually he came to an old yard with no name visible, just scattered scrap iron and old barges plus a big workshop, a crane and, beyond that, the River Thames.

The battleship HMS Belfast –
the type of vessel a naval architect would survey

Among the iron chaos, he found Mr Jack Hall, a man of seventy. At the time we thought that was old, but now it sounds young! He was darting around in his gumboots on the shingle. The tide was out and, sitting on the beach, was a barge, rusty and full of water. It looked knackered.

Mr Hall called out, "That's your boat". Gren answered, meekly, "Right". Then he was told that the yard would give us the boat if we gave them the work of repairing it, because it wasn't any use to them and wasn't worth much for scrap.

The Puppet Theatre Barge, 1981

The rusting back deck

Gren looked at the barge, an old Thames lighter named *Maybrent*, built around 1920. Mr Hall looked at him, waiting for a decision, and was kept waiting a full twenty seconds while Gren stood looking at the great hulk of metal. In that space of time he saw our touring stage in the barge, with some chairs and a canvas over the top, and the dawn of a new era presenting shows in our own theatre. He agreed to the deal.

Later Gren said that he was reminded of the first room he decorated for himself, when he was eighteen years old. As he set to with paint and brush, he had a vision of an amazing New York penthouse; of course, not being a professional decorator, the room ended up in a mess and it was a great disappointment. Well, the barge has never been like that. Because the initial vision was at such a simple level everything we've done since has only made it better.

Thomas Hughan's yard was situated exactly where the Millennium Dome was later built. Our starting point: an empty hull 75 feet long by 14 feet wide; approximately 1000 square feet of space. Enough for a fifty-seat theatre.

We can't thank Mr Jack Hall enough for what he did for us. He must have known what he was doing. One of those wonderful men you meet in a long life, he was obviously wise. What was to follow would be a very steep learning curve for both of us. Just a hull!

We both thought, "*Wow*". What a daunting task lay ahead. Then the yard took over and, unfortunately, they were completely inefficient. The politics of the country were in the same state, so one can't blame the yard management entirely. It was 1981 and Britain was changing. The left had been in the ascendant and now the right wing came into power with the "blessed Margaret" beginning to show her muscle. The yard, and the country, descended into anarchy. During the 1970s there had been a sea change in working practice and economics, which led to one strike after another, starting with Red Rob at British Leyland. Then came Mr Scargill, shop steward extraordinaire, and the coal miners! All of this turmoil was reflected in the practice at the yard.

The boss, a Captain Smith, gave us permission to work on the boat alongside a designated welder/fabricator. We used to go down regularly and work on the barge whenever we could; the yard was good about that. We were also very lucky with the man who was assigned to our boat. He was a very good craftsman and helped us enormously with the design and construction of all the elements. His name was Joe.

The work went on day after day, then week after week and finally month after month. It took us a while to realise the routine: at about quarter to one, the management would knock off and head for the pub in Greenwich. Then at ten to one, when the management had disappeared, the workers would start to knock off slowly, and by five to one they had broken up and everyone was out at lunch. When, at two o'clock, the hooter announced the end of the lunch hour, it was time to start work again. The workers would slowly drift back to their various stations. They would appear out of the canteen area, or wherever they were, and light a fag. Then they would stand about having a smoke before walking slowly to their place of work, so that by ten past two they were back on the job, so to speak. At quarter past two, the management would arrive back slightly tight, having had a couple of pints. The supreme boss, a Mr Potter, used to come down into the yard shouting at all the men to get on with the job, and then he'd shout at us, "Oi, bloody sissies down there!". Gren used to laugh because he thought Potter was taking the "Michael" – he didn't realise that he was actually serious. We heard later that he had previously worked on a police fraud squad and was subsequently caught in Portugal with the company Jaguar! How true that is we cannot be sure.

The staff thought we must be eccentric millionaires, two artistic Bohemian types messing about on a boat at Bugsby's Marsh (the old name for where the barge was moored). They just let us get on with it. Joe, our fabricator, was quite an odd chap – an accomplished welder with artistic ambitions who liked jazz. He didn't smoke, which was very unusual at that time, and was an advantage to us, because a guy who doesn't take smoke breaks is much more productive.

Gren and Juliet pause in between work

So, Joe was very innovative and was, we think, a frustrated artist. He helped so much with the detail: the hinging of the roof structure, the height of the raked seating and all sorts of things like that. Gren had drawn up a plan of what we wanted, but it was really Joe who converted that barge for us. It was serendipity to have met somebody like him.

The yard itself was another matter: inefficient and badly run. We suspected that the foreman would sign his son-in-law in as a freelance, on the weekend, when no boss was there. The son-in-law would get double time for Saturday and Sunday. He wouldn't be working for most of that time, but he'd be on the books.

The foreman was the only one allowed to work the crane that moved bottles of gas or other heavy items around the yard, but he was so completely uncooperative that Joe would have to waste three hours building some kind of prefabricated scaffolding structure to move gas or big bits of metal around on our barge. It was very frustrating.

Every so often we would say to ourselves that it was time to give the yard some money, as Joe had been doing a lot of welding and fabricating for us. Gren would duly go up to the office, which was the size of two kitchen tables. The secretary sat at a desk covered with papers – and we mean really covered. You could not see the top of the desk apart from a little space in front of her. The firm was so behind with all its invoicing it just did not know whether it was coming or going. In the end, this was to our advantage.

Chapter 4

The End of the Beginning

Mountains will go into labour,
and a silly little mouse will be born.
Horace *(65–8 BC)*
Ars Poetica

Prior to starting on the barge, Jack Hall had insisted that we have a proper survey conducted. He introduced us to Mr Woodvine, a surveyor from Canvey Island, who came up to London and gave our newly acquired barge the once over. He recommended that we cover the ceiling – the ceiling is actually the floor of a boat in Navy-speak – with a three-inch layer of concrete. His reasoning was that it would act as ballast and stabilise the vessel.

At the end of the day his advice was very good, but implementing his suggestion caused a lot of trouble. The order was given to the yard and a ready-mix cement lorry duly arrived and poured tons of concrete into the barge. The boat was moored out on the high water while the concrete set. Unfortunately, twelve hours later the tide went out and the boat came to rest on the beach that had a slight slope, as beaches do. It wasn't long before the concrete had slowly shifted to one side and hardened, leaving the boat

Gren contemplates

with a two-and-a-half-inch list to starboard, putting the vertical out of alignment. Not good for string puppets.

A long battle with the yard ensued. They kept saying, "We're getting a scabbler that'll take it out, don't worry". The concrete was getting harder and harder and the mythical machine never arrived. In the end we hired a Kango hammer and did quite a lot of demolition ourselves, but Gren wasn't strong enough to lift it all out.

Joe put in a sub-floor for us, compensating for the list. Then out of

The Interior of the barge after the concrete had dried

the blue we were offered some wonderful floor tiles, mounted on one-inch ply. Chris Spencer, a local Hackney councillor who was running Hackney Youth Workforce, had been offered them by a floor factory that was closing down, and he passed them on to us. It is wonderful how luck has played such a big part in our enterprise. Joe made the tiles fit his sub-floor and they are indestructible.

Chris also helped us by providing youth labour from the "Workforce". That was a lesson and a half! They were some wild kids! Mostly boys, but a couple of girls, showed up and we put them all on to painting and wire brushing the hull. None of them had much, if any, work experience and even managing a paint brush was testing – they would drop the brush in the mud and then dip it in the paint. Ouch! At lunchtime they would go and sit in our van – we didn't realise that they would finish one or two bottles of Martini during the break. We are talking about sixteen-year-olds. Once, when we had a touring job in Gloucester, we took the two girls with us. It was a total adventure for them, as we discovered en route that they had never been out of Hackney. After some weeks of working with the kids in the yard we finished up with a bit of prop-making, which was much more to their liking.

Joe, the wonder welder, was basically doing the construction single-

Joe keeps a perfect straight line while an apprentice looks on

handedly with odd help he'd get from other welders seconded to the barge. We would negotiate with Captain Smith, the yard manager, practically every day. Over a period of a year the inefficiency was slowly wearing us down, because progress was so slow. It was frustrating, but the theatre gradually took shape.

Finally, just before Christmas 1981, we were ready to "sheet up" – in other words, to put the canvasses on the barge that would enclose it. It was a bitterly cold year with early snow in December. We had arranged to have a mooring at Camden Lock, which was already a fashionable spot for Londoners and visitors alike. The market was attracting a growing number of trendy people to the area – in terms of potential audiences, this was more than we could have hoped for. The architecture of Camden was attractive, and the layout of the canal incorporated a small arm off the main channel. This was the perfect spot for our barge, secure and with easy public access. The two bosses of the market, Bill Fulford and Peter Wheeler, were pleasant, highly intelligent men who saw the potential of a puppet theatre in the centre of this busy, expanding area.

We had hoped to get to our mooring for the Christmas season of 1981. December came and went, and the New Year arrived. We decided to move the barge out of the yard and to finish the work as we went along. We started to prepare for the moment. This was quite a tricky time. We didn't realise just how paranoid the management was with regard to us moving the vessel.

Coincidentally, 36 years after the barge left the yard, the following email arrived out of the blue:

> *Hi*
>
> *I helped convert a small barge into a puppet theatre back in the 1980s at a small boat yard in Greenwich.*
>
> *Can this be the same barge?*
>
> *We got to know the couple quite well.*
>
> *Best regards*
>
> *Russell Debnam*

Gren replied and told him that it was indeed the same barge, and got some more details from Russell:

> *Hi Gren*
>
> *I was an apprentice engineer. I helped Joe Gillard (the steel fabrication engineer) cut the transom away and form the mounting for your drive motor.*

I helped install the control systems with the fitter foreman. We also waterproofed the hull by sealing the loose rivets, etc. We then fabricated a lot of what was needed to transform your vessel into the glorious theatre it is today. We also visited you on the canal to undertake some remedial works. I remember it was very icy!!

Today I have my own maintenance company, where I undertake various projects from fabrication of bespoke structures to specialist lifting equipment inspections.

Have you any photos from the yard?

Best regards

Russell

Our correspondence continued, and Russell sent his Apprenticeship Certificate, signed off by our very own Captain Smith.

Russell Debnam's signing-off certificate

Russell continued:

I actually stood on the quayside with Joe as you sailed off from T W Hughan's yard. Joe was so proud of the work he put into your project.

When I left Hughan's in 1982, I worked with Joe's brother Mike for a short while until I was offered a position in Erith as an engineer. I learnt a lot from Joe. I always thought he would get fed up with all my questions, but he was a very good craftsman and showed me many techniques that I still use today! I also caught his bug of loving jazz music – so much so that I played a trumpet in a band until my mid-twenties.

I got married in 1986 to my lovely wife Lisa. We have two children, Richard, 29 years old, and Mahala, who is 25 years old. My engineering studies continued, and I achieved my degree status in 1990 and my chartered status in 2012.

So, you both, the Puppet Barge Maybrent, Joe Gillard and Thomas W Hughan have all contributed to my now successful career!

Such is the influence the Puppet Theatre Barge has had over the years and continues to have today.

We needed to hire a tug. Our man Joe knew a fellow welder Paul Deverell, who worked on the river and had his own small yard on the Thames. Paul now has a massive yard and is a tough operator, but at that time he was just a young man and keen to get a job, as the previous year had seen quite a big recession. We were able to engage him, and he arranged a tug for the move. Gren arrived early in the morning on the designated day and remembers waiting for the tug. He had forgotten about the tide that seemed to take forever to rise up and float the barge. He knew the management was watching him as he pottered about the beach and boat trying to keep busy. At last the tide was up and the tug duly arrived. He threw the tug skipper a line and off went the barge, out of the yard. What an experience!

The barge is comprised of a lot of iron! At 75 feet long and 14 feet wide is quite big – fortunately the tug was in charge. Gren was on the back of the boat, supposedly steering it. However, the rudder, which

Captain Smith had designed, was much too small and thus completely useless. It was just Gren on board, as green as grass and with no form of contact with the tug that was towing the barge at a fair rate of knots. Inadequate is the word! Even so, the barge soon arrived at Limehouse, the entrance to the canal system.

Juliet was there to meet the barge, but it couldn't get into Limehouse Basin. The electric bridge, which was supposed to go up to let us in, wasn't working. It was frozen. Everything was frozen. The entire world of British Waterways was frozen. The canal people were frozen, and they even seemed pleased that the bridge wasn't working!

When you arrive at the wharf edge on top of the tide you can literally step off the boat, the equivalent of one step, onto dry land. As we were not able to get the barge into the basin at this point the tug man said, "Look, we'll take this boat away and moor it on a barge road". (A barge road is a line of barges on the Thames where boats are tied up on a temporary basis.) We were told to come back at low tide, which was at two o'clock in the morning, when he would bring the barge back and get it under the bridge and into Limehouse Basin without any trouble.

We went back home, had some dinner and dozed for an hour before returning to Limehouse. The tide was out and we looked for the barge. We could not believe our eyes when we looked over the side of the wharf and saw a little barge moored forty feet below us. It had been delivered as promised and Paul Deverell was on board. It was difficult to believe that the fall of the tide could make such a difference. There was no stepping onto the deck, but a rather scary experience of having to climb down using steps set into the side of the wharf. One had to step off into space to try and find the first rung. And we were doing this in the dark with everything frozen around us. Paul was there to help and encourage us when we had to take this first step off the side, into blackness. There was some feeble light from an office window, and we finally managed despite the icy conditions and the dark.

Paul was very good and helped us as we got down onto the barge that was hard aground on the riverbed. We could have taken a walk on that riverbed, but we waited patiently for the tide to rise and give us enough water to lift the barge and allow us to get into the lock.

In the yard, at some point we had installed a little well at the back of the barge where we could fit a small outboard engine. This was deemed good enough for moving us on the canal but proved totally inadequate on the Thames.

Paul started our little motor and was in charge as we were nosing around into the dock. He shouted to the British Waterways worker above, "OK, throw the rope down". The guy threw down the rope that was holding us, but just as he threw it the tide took the front of our boat – it took it and we couldn't catch hold of anything, we just kept moving away from the lock until we were travelling fast with the tide: no lights, completely out of control, heading upstream towards town.

The tiny engine just couldn't cope. It cut out, so there was nothing, absolutely nothing, to stop us. Gren is quite good in a panic moment, and quite brave as well, just a natural thing, so he got out a torch and flashed the Morse code SOS – dot-dot-dot, dash-dash-dash, dot-dot-dot. He had learned the code as a kid. We could see no boats … nothing and were travelling at a terrific speed. Juliet, hanging on to the front deck and dreading what we were going to collide with, could see we were coming up to a pub called the Prospect of Whitby, outside of which was moored a beautifully restored Thames wooden sailing barge. We thought: are we going to smash into it? As we passed we hit some iron barges on the side and literally, sparks came off them. Then we saw a boat in the distance and Gren kept flashing SOS as fast as he could. At last there was a response from a police launch. They came alongside, took in the situation and threw us a line. Once again Paul was good. He was able to talk their talk, a sort of butch river patois, and told them that our engine had broken down. He didn't tell them the size of it and the police didn't notice that we had no lights; in fact we didn't have any insurance, we didn't have anything! Anyway, they started to tow us back but they couldn't pull the barge against the tide, so they radioed for another launch. When the second boat arrived, we were finally towed back to Limehouse.

We got into the basin at about four in the morning. It was absolutely calm. We couldn't believe it; the quiet was just uncanny when we got off the river. And the police were very nice, except one aggressive youngster who was trying to pin something on us.

Gren, having grown up in South Africa, had learned a few things about confronting the police. He reckons if there are four or five policemen present you should look for the one with the different hat – he's the boss. You should then direct all your answers to him, with the occasional glance at the others. He has found this works all over the world, and even held true when he was confronted by some Syrian soldiers while filming in Lebanon. Whippersnappers always try to impress the boss, so if you're subservient to the boss but not to the others, you might get away unscathed.

Chapter 5

The First Journey

A cold coming we had of it
Just the worst time of the year
For a journey, and such a long journey
The ways deep and the weather sharp,
The very dead of winter.

T S Eliot

Journey of the Magi (1927)

Rather like the birth of an elephant, with its long gestation period, so was the birth of the Puppet Theatre Barge, struggling to cope with the demands put upon it. Ahead lay the six-mile journey to Camden Town.

On the morning following the Thames adventure we met up with Paul Deverell at Limehouse and found the barge tied up, floating serenely, in the calmest of waters. We, the proud owners of a large vessel, had no knowledge of how to navigate this new-born object.

Little did we realise then how many people on the canal have firm opinions on how to do things, and how positively they speak on such matters, so that what they say seems to be indisputable! Now, looking back, we cannot believe how much dud information we have been given over the years, but when you're a greenhorn you just accept the bull-dust as fact. A fine example of this occurred on our very first journey.

Having heard about the barge via river gossip, Warwick, a man known to Paul, turned up at our door. Warwick, who purported to know about the canal, had been loaned a small passenger boat by a Thames operator hoping to find out if there was any business potential for a small passenger boat on the canal. Warwick lived in a house backing on to the Hertford Union Canal, which, connecting the River Lea with the Regent's

Canal, was useful for the boat operators. We had planned to travel from Limehouse to Camden the straightforward way along the Regent's Canal, but Warwick wanted to make the journey via the River Lea and Hertford Union. He thought it best to go that way. What we did not know at the time was that Warwick had a hidden agenda! He wanted to get us to go that way, so he could impress the local councillor by bringing traffic onto the canal. At that time the Hertford Union was hardly used, and certainly no boats were to be found on the canal in mid-winter.

Warwick said to us, "Oh, go around via the Hertford Union. That would be much better". Being innocents we were convinced and followed his advice, going up the Lea and round and down the Hertford Union. That way took a lot of extra time. And as we set off everything became frozen: we became frozen, and the canal started to freeze until we were literally cutting through the ice and trying to break it up with a barge pole and a broomstick!

We had been making a production of *The Ancient Mariner* at the time and these words from the poem kept going through our heads:

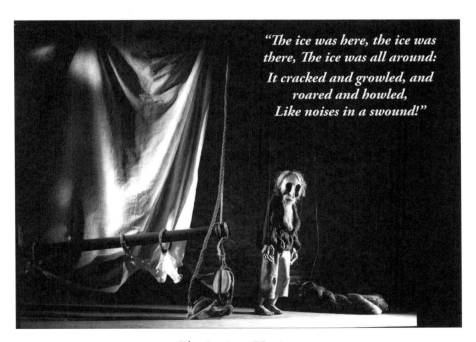

"The ice was here, the ice was there, The ice was all around: It cracked and growled, and roared and howled, Like noises in a swound!"

The Ancient Mariner

31

And that was exactly what it was like. Coleridge hit the nail on the head when he wrote those lines. Unfortunately, an albatross never did arrive to bring us any luck. We made it to Old Ford before becoming frozen in. The boat just would not move. It was like being in the Arctic.

However, while we were stuck at Old Ford we managed to do quite a lot of work. The lock-keeper offered us some power, so we ran a long cable from the lock office and Paul Deverell brought in his portable welders. We worked on the barge every day for two weeks. Paul fitted the portholes and finished off a lot of small jobs. Eventually the ice began to soften.

Old Ford Lock Cottage

We were desperate to get to Camden. Juliet struggled to find a call box, phoned British Waterways and asked for help. They responded and towed us through the melting ice. These were all new adventures to us, but luckily we had help on board – in addition to Paul there was Joe, who'd been with us in the yard and whom we were paying to be there. Having passed through the Islington Tunnel, which is nearly a mile long, British Waterways eventually moored us up at Battlebridge Basin close to King's Cross. That evening we had a visit from John Wright, accompanied by Bruce Schwartz, a famous American puppeteer who went on to operate the puppets in Krzysztof Kieslowski's 1991 film *The Double Life of Véronique*. He was interesting, and it was a privilege to meet him. *See footnote*

The following day British Waterways towed us to Camden Town and we learned what a "pound" on the canal is (the stretch of water between locks). That was about as much as we could take in. With our subsequent experience, both of us would say that it takes a four-year apprenticeship to learn how to handle the barge competently – a long time.

The barge was placed first not in the arm but in the mainstream of the canal against the wall just above the lock. British Waterways then left us to cope on our own. Paul did a few more jobs, and then he and Joe, too, were gone. We sorted out the tarpaulins and began to get the barge ready for the move across the canal into the arm. We were now solely in charge and had to manoeuvre the blessed boat ourselves. It is a huge vessel.

As it happened the distance from the wall to the wharf was not great, so we managed the move without any problem – other than mental stress! Once the barge was in the wharf we erected the roof, plugged into the mains, lit the coal-burning stoves that we had had installed, lit the brass lanterns and rigged the show. We were ready for an audience.

We actually opened on January 28, 1982, exactly a year after acquiring the barge. Through Kenneth Griffith, an actor friend of ours, we managed to acquire the services of Baron Miles of Blackfriars, the actor Bernard Miles, to perform the opening ceremony on that cold winter's day. We invited him because

Gren and Baron Miles of Blackfriars

he had created the Mermaid Theatre in a warehouse on the banks of the River Thames in the City of London, so we thought he was an appropriate choice. He made a good speech with some nice humour, saying he thought it useful that the theatre was small as it is very nasty if you have a big space and only a few people turn up for a show.

Juliet and Kenneth Griffith –
actor and filmmaker

Our tiny invited audience saw the very first performance of *The Ancient Mariner* that we had been making, usually at night, throughout the year while the barge was being converted. Somehow, when one is younger, it is possible to do these things; one just does them. We don't know how they come together but they do. It was very exciting. We had a very enjoyable opening with family and friends plus our main actor, Ken Griffith and puppet master John Wright, with Lyndie, his wife. Ken Griffith and Bernard Miles were both celebrities in the sixties. Baron Miles was born of working-class parents and was only the second actor to be awarded a peerage. Ken, well-known actor and filmmaker, and avid collector of Boer War memorabilia, died in 2006. His archive is with the Tenby Museum in Wales. John Wright died in 1991 at the age of 86. He was working until his death and left The Little Angel in prime order. It is a flourishing, world-famous theatre today.

The first public performance of the show, the following weekend, was almost an anti-climax. Although opening the show to the public was exciting we realised, very quickly, that the real season had started and that the job of securing an audience and facing the public was not going to be easy. It is a long learning curve finding out how to induce people into paying money to come and see a marionette drama!

After a year in the yard – a whole year – we were exhausted, but adrenalin was holding us together, which was a good thing. We had to face Captain Smith as he handed us a large invoice and wanted immediate payment. Gren thought this was outrageous as they had not done some of the work for which they invoiced us and there was absolutely no mention of, or apology for, the mess they had made with the concrete. We had a short discussion with Captain Smith but did not pay at the time. Mr Potter, the boss of the yard, immediately served a "Notice in Rem" – a naval term – on us. Such notices, served by the Admiralty Court, are usually stuck to the mast of a boat but in our case, with no mast, it was plastered on the door.

We would have honoured the debt in the end, but because they had not attempted to remedy or even say anything about the concrete and Potter had promptly plonked the writ on the barge, we countersued. We were able to do this because we had some wonderful legal advice from our friend Harry Hails, who worked for an important legal firm in the City.

*[**footnote 1**] *When coming to write this history, we remembered Bruce as having operated the puppets in the film* Being John Malkovich. *In researching this, Gren learned that in fact they were created by Kamela Portuges and animated by Phillip Huber. An interview with Huber by Steve Meltzer is published in* Puppetry Journal *(Fall 1999) under the title "Marionettes in Hollywood" — see www.hubermarionettes.com/bjm/bjminterview.html. Marionettists will be interested to read the following quote from Huber's interview: "The marionette work I've seen in films has been, for the most part, less than thrilling. Often, they are a gimmick, or a mere stand-in for human actors and they almost always appear under-rehearsed. Films have consistently failed to show marionettes to their best advantage." We at the Puppet Barge agree with him.*

Chapter 6

Preparations

Progress, therefore, is not an accident,
but a necessity ... it is part of nature.
Herbert Spencer
Social Statics (1851)

Following our opening weekend, we had to attend to a previously arranged touring date. This would have been easy before the barge opening, but now we had to take the stage out of the barge, pack it into the trailer and drive to Liverpool very early the following morning. We gave two performances, packed it all up again, and drove back to London. After two nights with practically no sleep at all, we got back in time to re-rig the stage on the barge, and to prepare and rehearse the show ready for the second weekend.

The Admiralty writ was hanging over our heads and something had to be done, so Gren turned to the bank. Many years before the writ was served, we had opened an account at the Baker Street branch of the National Westminster bank; dealings there were with the Assistant Manager, a Mr Mike Bowler. Mr Bowler was an angel sent from heaven! When he was promoted we moved our account across town to his new branch near Paddington Station. He never forgot our loyalty, and when Gren told him of the Admiralty writ and that, to persevere with the case, we would have to deposit the money invoiced plus £1000 to cover the court costs, he immediately agreed to advance the money to the court. And so the negotiations with the yard's solicitors began.

We had hardly cleared the way for the court action to commence and were continuing with the opening season of the barge, when a young man from Pakistan, Faizaan Peerzada, appeared on the scene with an exotic request. He asked us to go to Pakistan for a tour. His father had taken him and his twin brother to a marionette show when he was a young boy and he had never forgotten it; he wanted to offer the same experience to the next generation of children in his country.

Making arrangements with Faizaan was difficult. Once he was back in Pakistan, the only way of contacting each other was by barely audible phone conversations. No emails or texts in those days!

Juliet takes up the story:

"We had planned to take our marionette stage with lights, props, backdrops, etc, but at the last moment when all was packed for flying – no easy task – no money was forthcoming for excess weight so only puppets and props travelled with us. On arrival in Karachi, Gren went ahead to the venue with Faizaan to start building a stage out of various lengths of timber, with the help of a local carpenter. I stayed behind to guide the puppets and props through customs. Luckily, I had the help of Faizaan's glamorous older brother, a film star who was mobbed by adoring fans. He eased the way for us.

When we arrived at the site, the stage was half up, and the audience was entering the large tent specially erected for the performances. The show was due to start at 4pm but the curtain only went up at 8pm! No one seemed bothered by the delay; the audience watched as we put things together, eating and chatting happily. Finally, the show got underway and we were clapped and cheered during the parts of the show they liked. No applause at the end!

We were exhausted after travelling and performing but Faizaan's hospitality was wonderful, and we were looked after very well.

The next month took us north

Juliet and the finished stage

from Karachi by steam train to Lahore, where we stayed with Faizaan's big family. We then travelled by ox cart and wonderfully adorned lorries to other towns including Islamabad and Rawalpindi. The journeys were adventures in themselves, with Gren begging drivers to go more slowly and, on the odd occasion, actually paying them to do so! But never did we have to lift a box or carry a case; there were always willing hands to help and many onlookers gazing at us in amazement. Once we found ourselves in a Catholic boarding school run by nuns, with an audience of attentive uniformed girls who seemed to understand Shakespeare.

The three plays we took to Pakistan included *Monkey Business*, *The Birdman* and *Bottom's Dream*. Faizaan printed a poster offering all three plays on one ticket, but we refused to comply! Towards the end

The poster is about 13 feet high

of the tour we were performing in the Holiday Inn in Islamabad, and living quite luxuriously, when Faizaan announced, 'We have arranged just three more shows in Rawalpindi.' We just lay down on the thick pile carpet of the hotel and refused. After 24 shows in 27 days we were totally exhausted. Not just the travelling and performing but rigging and striking the stage had worn us out. I will always remember Faizaan's description of working with us, 'When you have been out on a show with Movingstage, every bone in your body says goodbye.'

In the end we agreed to the extra shows and went to that extraordinary ancient town of Rawalpindi and played in a glorious, ripped, colourful tent.

The country felt a lot more peaceful for travellers in those days, in spite of being under the dictatorship of Zia-ul-Haq. There was nothing like the tension in crowded places that there is nowadays. Lahore, in particular, is a beautiful town, especially the walled inner city, which hasn't changed since Biblical times. We left feeling connected to the place and, most of all, to the Peerzada family, with whom we are still in touch."

Faizaan's enthusiasm ultimately resulted in us performing 27 shows in 29 days, finishing in Rawalpindi before flying home. The experience was exhilarating – including the time when we ran away from a beggar. At least there were no Taliban about.

The tent where we performed in Rawalpindi

Meanwhile, during our time in Pakistan we invited an English puppeteer, Christopher Leith, to present his shadow show on the barge and John Alexander, Punch professor, to present his Punch and Judy show outside the barge. This stopped the theatre from going dark, but they struggled to get an audience.

Note our Birdman poster on a pillar

Following our return to England, our friend Harry had set our response to the Admiralty court writ in motion and arranged legal aid for us, which was a real blessing. Negotiations in earnest, went on for a year until the yard capitulated and settled out of court. All we had to pay were the fees owed to the yard's solicitors, which amounted to around half of the invoice total. All was well, and the barge belonged to us.

Having settled our debt with Thomas Hughan's boatyard we wondered whether the original barge owners, a Mrs Mary E Brook and Mrs Shirley Gilbert of Bargeletters Limited, would have been as harsh as Thomas Hughan!

The barge loaded with logs c. 1952

Chapter 7

First Year Apprenticeship

To travel hopefully is a better thing than to arrive.
Robert Louis Stevenson
Virginibus Puerisque (1881)

Towards the end of February 1982, soon after we had opened the barge, a Mr Rod Saunders visited us at Camden and invited us to go for a summer season at his newly created marina in Pitstone. This small village on the Grand Union Canal in Buckinghamshire, happens to be next to a mainline railway and very close to where the Great Train Robbery had taken place nearly twenty years before. Today the stolen money would be equivalent to £49.1 million – at the time, 1963, it was a mere £2.6 million. We accepted this invitation gladly, as we had always planned to take the theatre to other locations during the summer; our immediate concern, however, was the Pakistan trip planned for March.

Gren takes up the story:

"Before we could undertake the journey into the heart of Bucks we had to fit a bigger engine into the barge. Lighters like ours had always been referred to as 'dumb barges' as they had never been fitted with engines and were originally horse drawn.

To this end I managed to persuade a friend, Nigel Morgan, to help me with this new project. In the late spring of 1982, after our return from Pakistan, we took the barge back to Old Ford, in Victoria Park, for a festival. Chris Spencer of the Hackney Youth Workforce was partly involved with the running of the event and tried his best to get an audience for us by standing on the bridge with a loud hailer and repeating the words, 'Magic and fantasy … magic and fantasy … magic and fantasy …'.

After the festival we moored up alongside the Cricketers pub and Nigel and I started on the engine installation. Some weeks before I had bought *Exchange and Mart*, a magazine devoted to hundreds of classified ads selling goods. In it I found a Perkins diesel engine and an Enfield Z Drive. I drove up to Birmingham and bought both, whereupon Nigel and I began the task of fitting them in the barge. Not an easy job.

Barges being towed, c.1950; Maybrent can be seen at the back

Following the completion of the barge work I was offered, luckily, a film, and was away in India for about six weeks where I photographed a documentary on Clive of India and made some money to keep us going. During my absence Juliet was planning the tour up the Grand Union Canal to Pitstone, arranging different spots where we could moor and present our show. She also made contact with schools at Pitstone and managed to book sixteen school performances. At the same time, with the help of our artist friend David Welsh, she put up posters around Pitstone and Tring advertising the tour.

After a debriefing upon my return to England and intensive preparation of the barge, we set out on the planned journey. Our first day's travel took us to Kensal Green Cemetery and we arrived at Old Oak Common for the first night, thinking that we were miles from London when in fact we were only just west of centre!"

The short journey through west London was a baptism of fire, from which we soon learned that we would need help from a third person. After finding a phone box, a miracle of the past, Juliet managed to persuade puppeteer/historian George Speaight to join us. George was not only involved in puppetry, having written the definitive *The History of the English Puppet Theatre,* but was also a canal enthusiast. The next day we motored as far as the Black Horse pub at Greenford where we stayed overnight and picked up George in the morning. He helped us through the next day and then we managed to get a replacement in the form of our artist friend, David Welsh, who stayed with us for the rest of the journey.

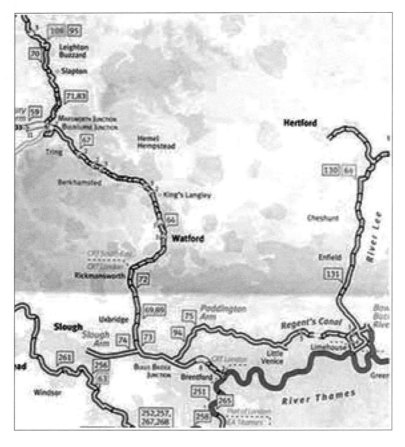

An old map showing our journey as far as Watford on the Grand Union Canal

The following day we got to Bull's Bridge, turned right onto the Grand Union, going towards Watford – and immediately ran aground. Thank goodness David was a strong man and could push and pull like an ox. While we were grappling to get going again, a voice from the towpath shouted, "You need a barge pole!" This was our first meeting with Tim Wood, a marine engineer and canal buff, who was to have a great influence on the barge. He came into the picture again the following year.

Still innocent, we struggled on through Cowley, getting stuck often. We arrived at a lock that we could not open and made contact with canal engineer Mr Patterson, who we subsequently christened "Dredger" Patterson. Despite the fact that he lived in the lock cottage, very close by, which is where we found him, he was rather late getting to us.

"Dredger", we decided, was definitely not pleased to see a barge the size of *Maybrent* being brought up the canal, drawing attention to the failures on the system – from lock gates that would not fully open to shallow sections in need of dredging. Although the locks on this section of the canal network were designed to accommodate wide barges such as ours, very few were now using the system. There were quite a few narrow boats, but they had no trouble getting through; their draft was less and only one lock gate needed to be opened at each end for them to pass through. So, in Dredger's opinion we were "a bloody nuisance and shouldn't be on the canal, especially with such a daft cargo!"

Just before we got underway he stated that we were too wide to get through a particular bridge hole. We had done our research with the British Waterways' office, however, so plodded on regardless, pushing and pulling and mooring overnight either outside the odd pub or beside a meadow.

On the fifth day we had travelled as far as Watford when we got our rudder caught in the lock gates and as the water rose the rudder bent. We freed the boat and pulled in to the canal side above the lock. Like a miracle, two goblins arrived out of the trees to help us. They were railway engineers on strike and asked us what the matter was. They disappeared, arriving back with a portable welder and tools, and set about fixing the rudder. Having done the job, they disappeared once more, never to be seen again!

The next day we had been going an hour or two when the engine stopped for no reason at all. At this point we thought we would not make it to Pitstone and worried about not being able to fulfil the agreements with the various schools. Still determined, we formulated a plan. Gren cycled down the canal to find boat expert James MacDonald, who lived not far away.

Gren continues:

"I found his boat and left a message explaining the problem and asking if he could come and find us. A couple of hours later he arrived at the barge. Being a Scottish engineer, he found the problem within minutes. 'Water in the diesel', he announced, in his broad accent. Further back down the canal we had unsuspectingly bought some diesel fuel with water in it. A bad deal! After that James was a friend for life and surveyed the barge for a safety certificate every four years until he retired thirty years later. Sadly, we lost touch."

Continuing our journey, we found no improvement in the canal, and shallow water continually held us up. At Apsley, where the Croxley Paper Mill was situated, it was so bad that we could hardly move forward at all. Seeing our predicament, a couple in a narrow boat stopped and helped by towing us for a fair distance, past the British Waterways' works at Bulbourne then all the way to the Tring summit. At last there was a fair amount of water and the flight of locks was easy going.

The walkway

We finally arrived at Pitstone wharf only to discover that the marina was far too shallow for us, so we moored up on the main canal instead. We had to run a power line from the marina shed a good 200 yards away. Fortunately, Rod Saunders had a stack of duckboards, so we were able to make a path from the marina buildings to the barge along the muddy bank.

We settled down for the summer and managed to get a fair attendance from the public, playing *The Birdman* and *Monkey Business* at the matinees and *The Ancient Mariner* on Saturday evenings. David helped with front of house (FOH) duties.

Note the health and safety entrance!

Heading back along the canal, we found that our earlier experience helped. We also stopped at various other locations that Juliet had arranged, mostly pubs, where we set up and presented short seasons. We finally arrived back in Camden six weeks later, completely exhausted, after the almost impossible task of navigating that stretch of water with such a big barge.

On top of all these barge and touring shenanigans, Gren was still doing little bits of film work to earn some money. In between jobs he was signing on, National Insurance keeping us from starving! Someone once said, "Do you know what the best sound in the world is?" Gren responded, "No, what is that?" The answer, "It's the sound of the National Insurance giro floating down from the letterbox to the floor." In those days social security money was paid via a giro in the post.

While we were in Camden, we were getting to know Bill and Peter who owned and developed the market and who were decent to us. Bill was a lecturer at Cambridge University and Peter had a leisure centre down in Cornwall. Under the name of Northside Developments, these two guys ran the whole of the Camden Lock site, which was a conglomeration of unused old work sheds and warehouses. They had created the whole scene out of a group of decaying, semi-derelict buildings and changed the face of Camden. The mooring there lasted a couple of years until the waterbus arrived, started and operated by the market owners.

Chapter 8

Foolhardy Optimism

If way to the Better there be, it exacts a full look at the Worst.
Thomas Hardy (1840-1928)
Profundis In Tenebris II (1902)

After our experience of the 1982 tour, for some extraordinary reason we took on a second tour the following year. 1983 saw the official start of the internet and this was followed by the first mobile phone call. This mobile invention did not reach Britain for another three years.

The lack of power and a telephone line had been a huge problem for us, both on tour and while moored at Camden Lock, and we realised that the theatre would not be viable without them. We had managed to draw power from the lock cottage at Camden, as it was not in full use or being let out; at the time British Waterways could not decide what to do with it. This, however, was not a permanent solution.

Northside Developments, had a small ground-floor office where Cathy Palmer, who acted as secretary for Bill and Peter, worked. Fortunately, these three were all very fair and helpful, and gave us permission to install a phone connection in their office. Gren ran a wire across the yard to the barge. This was not entirely satisfactory, as we also had a phone at home but could not divert calls to the barge – at any one time a person trying to make a booking would not know which number to ring.

We battled our way through the 1982/1983 winter season and were relieved when spring appeared, followed by our second canal tour. This time we were armed with one year of bitter experience and were actually looking forward to the experience. On the previous tour we had parted company with David Welsh, whose unreliability had got too much for us to manage. At a later date he did, however, paint some beautiful backdrops for us. This year we were joined by Steve Sharples as a trainee puppeteer. He was a university friend of our daughter Kate, and a real asset. Steve went on to become a puppeteer himself and much later started the very successful Treasure Trove Puppet Company.

Steve was such a helpful and friendly young man that he even had the approval of Gren's mother, Kath, who had come over from South Africa to England for a visit and stayed with us on the barge for a few weeks. Gren was pleased to see her, although they had had their differences during his childhood! Kath was in her seventies by then but remained the same unbending imperialist that she had always been, raised by a Victorian English aristocrat father, her mother having died when she was four years old. Gren was convinced that she thought of him as a bit of a waster. She never quite understood the film business and freelancing; like a lot of mothers she would have preferred her son to become a professional of some sort – an architect or lawyer for instance – so when he showed no talent in that direction he must have been something of a disappointment. But both of us were very pleased that she was genuinely impressed and proud of the puppet theatre. It was interesting that this old traditionalist liked the fact that it was a going concern; it looked substantial. It was fun and rewarding to think that the experience of the barge was a turning point for her. Gren believed his mother now recognised where his talents lay and that he knew how to use them.

We did have our struggles getting up to Pitstone and back again, but the main problem that hit us was financial. It was a particularly hot summer and houses were anything but full. We just weren't bringing in enough money in ticket sales to keep the barge afloat and ourselves as well.

Juliet recalls the problems well:

"The answer seemed to be in renting out our house and living on the barge all year round. We had become quite accustomed to this way of life during the summer tours. However, we then quickly realised that it would not be possible to stay on board over the winter, so where could we live?

Having seen a showman's wagon advertised for sale in *World's Fair*, we set off to Bedford to take a look. It was owned by one Mrs Smith, an elderly lady who had been in the fairground business all her life but had recently been persuaded to move into a small bungalow by her scrap merchant sons. She gave us tea in fine china cups and asked us why we wanted the wagon. We explained our circumstances and after a bit more questioning, she offered to show it to us. We liked it

For details write Box 103
World's Fair, Oldham OL1 4BB

FOR SALE
22ft. SHOWMAN'S LIVING WAGON
in need of restoration.
Underworks are sound.
£450 o.n.o.
**Phone Bedford 65400
after 6 p.m.**

Advertisement for the wagon in World's Fair, the newspaper designed for showmen

at once. It was traditionally built, with an A-bar at the front for towing by a lorry, and had what Mrs Smith described as 'mollycroft' windows and 'belly' boxes. Mollycroft windows are narrow rectangular glass panels built in a narrow line into the roof section, similar to those seen in old-fashioned railway carriages. The belly boxes, meanwhile, used for storing gas cylinders and other large items, were located under the floor, accessed from outside. She showed us around and asked us if we were handy. This, we soon learned, was because the roof leaked and needed treating with a sheet dipped in white lead. It sounded pretty ominous, but as the roof

The wagon being transported

was not that big an area we judged we could deal with it. By the time we were shown everything, including the best places to hide money, we had made up our minds.

We purchased the wagon for £450 and arranged to move it to London on a low loader. We kept in touch with Mrs Smith for many years, exchanging Christmas cards and news. She was always hoping we had 'had a good season' and understood our way of life.

The deal was done, and it wasn't long before the wagon was on its way to London.

We had arranged a small space for the wagon behind the Metropolitan Workshops, near our Hackney house, and set up home in it. We let out our house to young friends of our daughters, fresh from university, and had a friendly relationship with everyone. This allowed us to use the facilities for bathing and washing clothes. At the same time, we rented a small workshop in the Metropolitan, an old hospital on the Kingsland Road, so that we could continue carving puppets and making new shows. We installed a coal-burning stove in the wagon which kept us warm and was excellent for cooking. A year later we moved the wagon into the garden of our house, which was a step up as we were able to draw power from the building and had a phone line."

Home for a year or two

Chapter 9

Touring Up the River

There is nothing – absolutely nothing – half so much worth doing
as simply messing about in boats.

Kenneth Grahame

The Wind in the Willows (1908)

We were on the last leg of the 1983 tour when we met Tim Wood of Bull's Bridge fame. He had seen our struggles on the first tour and offered his services, for a price of course, to install a "proper" engine and drive in the barge. Having suffered two tours with the old Perkins and Z Drive we said we would consider it. Not long after, while we were in our space in the Met workshops, we received a call from Mark Eynon, director of the Henley Festival, inviting us to perform there; this set both our minds off into a furious thought process. Imaginative plans were made immediately, as a booking like this would require some very clear thinking and planning.

During this period our daughters were at university and returned home during holidays to live with their friends who had rented rooms in our house; they also gave their unstinting support to us and the barge, working front of house, taking bookings and so on. They were always reliable and understanding when we were working.

In the early spring of 1984 we showed Mark Eynon the barge. He had little knowledge of our operation but as he was running a festival right by the Thames, he was keen to include river activities. His introduction – on a bleak day, with an audience of Russian Jewish refugees, watching a show about an old man rescuing a small bird that had fallen out of a nest – did not impress him. The festival audience at Henley could not have been more different from the one we were performing for. That might have been the end of the matter, but Juliet managed to persuade him to come on a return visit. She recalls:

"Fortunately, on his second visit we were performing *Sir Gawain and the Green Knight* to our regular public, who responded warmly. The atmosphere in the barge must have convinced Mark that here was a unique theatre offering marionette productions, an unusual art form, in a sophisticated manner. He booked us for the festival."

Having come to an arrangement with Mark, we had to consider the matter of getting the barge up to Henley, navigating the tidal Thames, a whole different kettle of fish. The immediate problem was the inadequate engine. To this end we made contact again with Tim Wood, who we had discovered was a partner in T & D Murrell Marine. The company had canal premises at Adelaide Dock in Southall, on the Grand Union Canal, approximately halfway between Bull's Bridge and Brentford where the canal joins the Thames.

We discussed our requirements for a river expedition in more detail and received a written quote for the installation of a marinised Ford diesel engine and Volvo hydraulic drive. The cost was £6000 – about £13,500 in today's money. This seemed an enormous amount; at the time it could have bought a brand-new Austin Mini with leather seats!

We turned to our banking godfather, Mr Mike Bowler, who offered us a business development loan, known as a BDL to those in the know. We then arranged for Murrell Marine to install the necessary engine and drive.

We finished our winter season at Camden and headed off down the canal, turning left at Bull's Bridge, towards Adelaide Dock, a fresh experience after our previous Bull's Bridge encounters. It was new ground once again, finding our way to the dock. Although one can't get lost on the canal, the tension when travelling on new water is always there. We arrived as arranged, docked the barge and set off home by train from Southall with wobbly sea legs. All too easy!

It wasn't long before we met Tam and Di – the Murrells. Di was a formidable waterways woman with a lot of canal experience and Tam, her partner, was a gentle, thoughtful man with probably the same amount of experience. Tim Wood, our engine man, declared that he may have failed his A levels but at least he had written the exams! In fact, what Tim

Entrance to Adelaide Dock, Southall

offered, along with his marine engineering skills, was great enthusiasm, interest and innovation; it is doubtful whether good exam results would have made any difference to them.

During the installation of the engine and other works, back in London, we were busy changing the *Gawain* puppets from rod marionettes into string ones. When we first conceived the show, we had Italian-style medieval puppets in our thoughts, as used by the Sicilian puppeteers. After touring the show, we found that operating with rods did not offer enough subtlety of movement.

Our living conditions in the wagon were primitive, to say the least. The fire in the stove would go out overnight. By the morning it was freezing, and Gren was often to be seen in the Met yard scrabbling around for bits of kindling. However, our small workshop space was adequate and so slowly the puppets were made ready, the wagon roof repaired and reports on the engine installation were positive. We started to look at maps of the River Thames and began to get nervous at the realisation that navigating the river was not going to be chicken feed!

After a visit to Adelaide Dock, worry slowly crept in about the forthcoming Thames journey. We alleviated it slightly by procuring, through Tam, the services of one Andy Farquharson to pilot us up to Henley. Andy had, in the past, skippered Salter's passenger boats on the Thames and knew both the route and the river intimately. The day eventually dawned when the engine installation was complete, and we were ready to sail. Gren did comment to Tim that we could have bought a Mini Cooper for the money he charged us; his retort was that we would not be able to take a theatre upriver in a Mini. Quite correct, we thought.

Chapter 10

Ignorance

If one does not know to which port one is sailing,
no wind is favourable.
Seneca The Younger *(c. 4 BC–AD 6)*
Epistulae Morales

We set off from Adelaide Dock towards the Thames with Tim on the tiller, Andy and Tam next to him. Looking on helplessly and somewhat nervous were Juliet, Susan Beattie – friend, lodger and new trainee – and Gren.

Excitement mounted as the new engine and drive took us onto a new stretch of canal, heading towards Brentford and the tidal Thames, which is under the management of the Port of London Authority. In theory, you can travel by boat from New York to Birmingham without touching land; we only had to get to Henley which, at the time, seemed just as big a journey to us greenhorns.

We passed Norwood Top Lock, and proceeded to the Hanwell Flight, a series of locks taking us downhill towards the Thames and sea level. After four to six hours of canal slog we arrived at Thames Lock, the gateway to "big" water. It is a unique experience coming off the canal and entering the river. At this point the water becomes alive with power and the astonishing force of the tide. If you know the river you understand that you must use this force and work with it, otherwise you will be fighting a losing battle and wasting energy. Timing is everything. The body pumps out adrenalin at the very moment the barge emerges onto the river and the brain activates unknown messages, rather like a dream, that trigger fight or flight responses, as well as sheer excitement. We

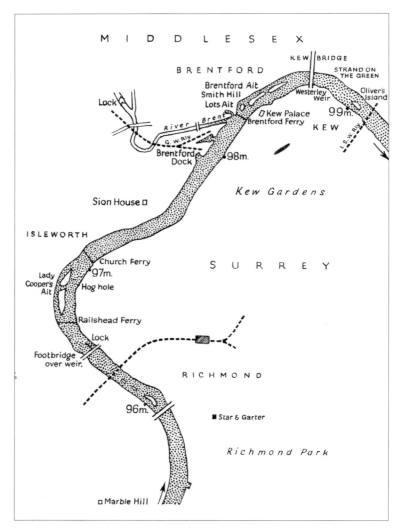

MIDDLESEX

BRENTFORD

KEW BRIDGE

STRAND ON THE GREEN

Brentford Ait
Smith Hill
Lots Ait

Westerley Weir

Oliver's Island

Lock

River Brent

G.W.Rly

Kew Palace
Brentford Ferry

99m.

KEW

L.S.W.Rly

Brentford Dock

98m.

Kew Gardens

Sion House

ISLEWORTH

SURREY

Church Ferry

97m.

Lady Cooper's Ait

Hog hole

Railshead Ferry

Lock

RICHMOND

Footbridge over weir.

96m.

Star & Garter

Richmond Park

Marble Hill

*The start of the journey from where the canal enters the
Thames at Brentford*

experienced all these sensations for more than two hours until we reached
Teddington Lock, where we said goodbye to Tim, Tam and tidal water.
We were comforted by the presence of Andy Farquharson, who had so
much confidence that practically all our worries disappeared.

We now know that to take the barge from Little Venice to Brentford,
through Thames Lock onto the Thames and then up to Teddington
Lock, takes two days; it takes a car about an hour. A completely useless

statistic, but nonetheless interesting from a logistics point of view, as it illustrates why canal transport gave way to the road.

At Teddington we came off the tidal section and entered the upper Thames, which is very well managed, with lock-keepers dressed in smart livery who keep the locks in an even smarter naval order. Teddington is a very big lock, capable of accepting a fair-sized ship. The river used to be part of the Port of London all the way up to Staines, but the Authority's jurisdiction now ends just below Teddington Lock. In Roman times the river was tidal as far up as Staines. In those days it was much wider and shallower; over the years it's been slowly dammed to make it far narrower, with locks controlling the fast-flowing water.

It took Andy approximately eighteen hours of motoring at full throttle to get us from Teddington to Henley. We had an overnight stop at Staines and then he made us rise at dawn and work the locks by hand! Andy proceeded relentlessly, chain-smoking roll-ups, having borrowed Sue's full packet of Golden Virginia – which she never saw again. We learned that his girlfriend was Minah Bird, a model and actress whom Gren had photographed some years back. Her name stuck in his memory.

Andy left us on our own, in a hyped-up condition, just above Hambledon Lock, below the Henley Royal Regatta course. The lock-keeper, a Mr Svenson, was a handsome man with an eye patch; his appearance caused us all to stand to attention! We got to know him

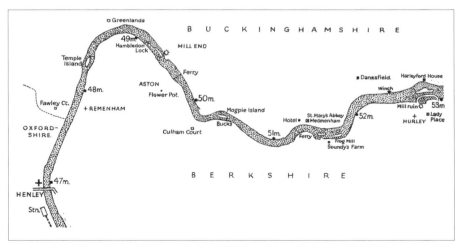

The Regatta course is one clear straight mile from Temple Island to Henley Bridge

over the years, and he always gave good advice on navigating the Regatta course. The Henley Royal Regatta takes place before the arts festival every year and so, after our first year of initiation, we knew to allow at least five to six days for the journey from Little Venice to Henley to ensure that we would arrive in time for the Regatta.

Looking towards Henley from our temporary mooring, prior to the festival, in the distance we could see the outline of many tents and a grandstand. There were people walking to and from Hambledon to the Regatta grounds and the starting post for the boat races. From this point, because the river has a straight run for a mile upstream, the place has become a mecca for scullers.

Not long after we were moored up we decided to take a walk into town. The walk seemed very long and as we got closer to the tents, voices of the hundreds of visitors got louder and louder. We watched an "eights" race as it passed by, the rowers all neck and neck, fighting for the winning place. The hoi polloi on the banks of the river were shouting and cheering, and by the time the boats were level with the grandstand the crowd was delirious. The noise hit a crescendo as the rowers crossed the finishing line and a moment later a hush came over the stand until the winner was announced.

Following the Royal Regatta, which lasts a few days, the tents are converted into restaurants, galleries and theatre and cabaret venues for the Henley Festival. Large sculptures are displayed around the festival grounds and there are busking theatricals, mime artists and acrobatic acts. At our first festival, Andrew Logan displayed his fantastic sculpture *Pegasus: Monument to Hope*. Andrew's brother Richard was his assistant. During the eighties, these two were also responsible for the Alternative Miss World competition, a clever gay send-up of the real thing.

The Henley Festival of Music and the Arts is a smart, fashionable event, attended by affluent types; the men in black dress suits and bow ties, the women in evening dresses. The doors opened at 6pm and from then until sometime after midnight people would promenade through the grounds while the festival management prayed that it would not rain. The barge gave two performances each night at the water's edge for fourteen years, at which point both we and the artistic director decided enough was enough.

In the months before our first festival performance we were introduced to the Leander Club, where we attended a press conference before the event started. The presence of the media saved us from being swamped by the very elite atmosphere that the club presented. Founded in 1818 on the south bank of the Thames, it was a London club described by Lord Esher in the nineteenth-century as:

"consisting of men who had never been at the University but were recognised throughout England, and perhaps everywhere in the world, as the finest rowers who had up to that time been seen."

This description befits the club, which moved to Henley in 1897, to this day. The only bad mark it deserves is for waiting until 1998 to open its doors to women.

At the club we met Tom Boswell, the chairman, and Jeremy Randall, the secretary. Both were unforgettable gentlemen and really helpful. Each year we would perform a season for the Henley townsfolk following the festival, mooring the barge outside the club and drawing our power from there. They granted us this favour for the many years that we ran our Henley town seasons. Another Henley gentleman was Richard Goddard, the secretary of the Royal Regatta, who gave us a mooring on regatta land for a very small fee.

During the years we moored at the club, we would watch England's top rowers, including gold-medal winners Matthew Pinsent and Steve Redgrave, launch their boats from the pontoon next to us and slip away downriver with a smooth, silent glide.

For our first year, both at the festival and for the town season, we presented *The Ancient Mariner* on Saturday evenings and *Monkey Business* for matinee performances. At the end of July, we left Henley and moved the barge to Marlow for a month, a pattern we were to follow for the next fourteen years, presenting, of course, different productions each year. The pattern changed slightly after we finished appearing at the festival.

Although Marlow is only eight miles from Henley, it has a completely different atmosphere. Henley has old money with many old people, and is in Berkshire; Marlow, in Buckinghamshire, is peopled by new money and younger families. Both towns have their own tastes in clothing, restaurants and shops.

Trapeze monkey

We researched Marlow after receiving the invitation to go to Henley and we managed to arrange a mooring in Higginson's Park. Our power came from a cottage on the edge of the park, facing the river. The kind elderly couple living there allowed us to plug into the socket in their garage. This facility lasted for a few years until we managed to share the installation of a power source close to the river with the organisers of the Marlow regatta. Gren still had to run a power line from tree to tree to the water's edge and then run the cable along the bed of the river. Although the installation was safe it didn't look it! The terrible procedure of climbing trees went on year after year for about twenty of our 25 years as the residential puppet theatre of Marlow.

All our Marlow arrangements were made through Wycombe Council, which liked the smell of money and so would charge us rather high fees. Fortunately, audiences were very good, as the park attracted a lot of people in the summer. Sometimes Carters Steam Fair would spend a season in the park which, in addition to bouncy castles and a permanent children's playground, contributed to the barge's success. We were privileged to meet Joby Carter, the founder of the fair, and to take an interesting tour of the showmen's wagons and the steam engines that ran the roundabouts and rides.

After a long four-week August season, the leaves would begin to turn yellow and we would move on to the next mooring. That varied over the years – sometimes it was Cliveden or Windsor – before we ended up in Richmond. In the early days we would take the barge as far as Oxford and play in places such as Abingdon, Wallingford, Caversham, Goring and further on downstream. We had good times and bad.

We quite often had minor engine breakdowns, when we would have to call on an expert to get us going again. These were worrying times as we were always mindful of when the next show was due to open and lost time is stressful. In this respect we could not have had better help and support than from Steve Strickland, a marine engineer who came out whenever we broke down on the river or canal. Steve understood our need to get to the next mooring quickly, and he saved us on many occasions. Usually the breakdowns were due to clogged or failing cooling systems, or sometimes electrical faults which messed up the starter or pumps. Gren became pretty handy at dealing with the problems in their initial stages, but beyond a certain point we relied on Steve. Later we acquired a second boat, for accommodation, and sometimes we towed one or other of the boats for a few hours, to cover distance until he could reach us. We still rely on Steve and he regularly comes to service *Maybrent* before we set off on the river. He will be heard to say, "She's a very old girl you know, but I'll do what I can to keep her going". Thanks Steve, we'd be lost without you – and please don't retire without training somebody to take over. Like cars, boat engines have become high-tech and computerised, but not *Maybrent*. She's old and traditional, and fewer and fewer people have the skills to maintain her. Steve's invoices are detailed and act rather like a description of his day. For example:

> *Drove to barge, took 2 hours and then parked, paid..........£*

> *Went to get parts, took 1 hour but had to go elsewhere so took 2 hours. Parts...£*

Interesting and often funny, like *A Day in the Life of Steve Strickland*. We would end up paying the bill in quite a good mood, which is rare.

The barge has tested us over the years and by the end of our first Thames tour in 1984 we were worn out. We made our way back to Camden not knowing what to expect.

Chapter 11

Money

If possible, honestly, if not, somehow, make money.
Horace *(65–8 BC)*
Epistles

When we arrived back in Camden, we found ourselves pushed out of the lock yard and onto the main canal; it was not satisfactory, but we did the best thing we could and moored against the wall at the foot of the famous Camden Lock market bridge. It meant we had to run our gangplank right onto the front of the barge, which was unsuitable, but the show must go on and we managed to run the theatre at this spot.

We opened with a double bill, presenting *The Magic Box* followed by *More Monkeys* for the second half. Our records show that on Saturday October 27, 1984, we had an audience of four adults and seven children at noon, and thirteen adults and fourteen children at the afternoon show. In retrospect this was not shameful. There was no internet or website to publicise the shows in those days, but there were three listings magazines: *Time Out, City Limits* and *What's On.* We received good reviews from all of them, although our bank manager Mr Bowler did forward one that told us off for a safety aspect on the barge, which we later corrected.

In the spring of 1985 we acquired, for the staggering amount of £4000, a mobile phone bought on hire purchase. In the first quarter of the 21st century the equivalent value of that amount is in the order of £15,000. Calls were very expensive at the time, but the mobile phone was exactly what was needed in order to run a theatre on a barge. It did take another two years at least for the system to become half-way reliable and four years to pay off the bill. Now that mobile technology has advanced so far we hardly use a landline – we can take bookings in the office, at the barge, on the move and in many different locations as we go about the business of running a theatre. It is hard to believe that our first mobile cost so much.

We managed to keep the run going at Camden until April 1985 when we moved to Little Venice for a few weeks and continued with the same presentation through to early June. After this it was up anchor and onto the Thames, where we made for Chertsey Bridge Festival. Juliet continues:

"Our experiences with Andy Farquharson the previous summer had been a very good introduction to navigating the Thames and we felt reasonably confident as we came off the canal at Brentford and swept out onto the tidal waters.

The first part of the journey, as far up as Kingston, was straightforward, although we could feel a very strong current flowing against us, making our journey upriver hard going. This was not tidal force but land water, pouring down from the Cotswolds and gathering momentum as every tributary fed in. It had been exceptionally wet in the previous weeks and we soon realised that this was going to be a totally different journey from the previous summer.

Our first stop was Chertsey, where we had been invited to give a weekend of performances as part of a festival to celebrate the bicentenary of Chertsey Bridge. As we approached the town, coming through Shepperton and Sunbury, we felt the huge force of the current. We came under the bridge and just managed to stop the barge against the downward flow and tie up. We had an excellent weekend of shows and made ready to leave on Monday morning. As Gren gave the order, 'Cast off', the front of the barge moved out into the stream, but the aft end was aground and stuck in the mud. With full throttle we came free but now the front had swung round, being pushed by the current, and we found ourselves broadside across the river and being pushed fast towards the bridge. There was nothing we could do except hang on. The three of us, Sue, myself and Gren, braced ourselves as we smashed up against the centre arch of the bridge, with water pouring up all along the port side as the river roared down against us, pinning us to the bridge. At this moment our mobile phone rang and Sue, casually, took a booking as if nothing had happened. Fortunately, the person on the other end of the line could not see the booking office!

After what seemed like ages, a young man in a motorboat came out from Bates Boatyard and shouted, 'Are you taking on water?' None of us had thought to go below, so I rushed down and quickly decided all was dry and no damage done below decks. Eventually a powerful tug came and pulled us off and towed us up to Chertsey Lock, just above the bridge. Here we were questioned by the police and interviewed by the press. All in all, we survived with the loss of a bike, the side steps for access and a few other objects which the river claimed. We were shaken up but could not help having a wry smile at the irony of celebrating the building of Chertsey Bridge and then knocking chunks off it.

The rest of the journey was uneventful, but a long hard struggle. Some locks had a red warning notice up, preventing leisure craft from navigating. We, being a working boat, continued on. The worst points were just below the locks where the weirs feed into the river; Hambleden and Mapledurham were particularly difficult, and we had to make full throttle 'charges' across the foaming water to avoid getting swept off course. Finally, we made it to Sandford Lock, just below Oxford, utterly exhausted but triumphant."

The attraction of Sandford was The Kings Arms, a pub very popular with the locals and a pleasant place to moor. Here we continued presenting *The Magic Box,* which was turning out to be real magic, sustaining such a long run – which wasn't finished yet!

Back in London, we had been carving and preparing a new show for grown-ups and older children: *The Butterfly's Evil Spell,* written by García Lorca when he was eighteen years old.

Scorpy confronts the Ladybird

The characters in the play are beetles, ladybirds, a scorpion and, of course, the butterfly. It is an intense love story between the boy beetle and the butterfly. After performing it a good many times, we finally realised that Lorca was telling the world that he could not fit in with the inflexible social conventions of that time in Spain. In 1936, during the Spanish Civil War, Lorca was executed by Franco's fascist regime for this very fact. The manuscript of the play was found hidden in a haystack.

We first performed *The Butterfly's Evil Spell* at Sandford, on June 22, 1985, to a full house. We hasten to add that none of the public were friends! From Sandford we went on to Henley Festival and then to the Leander Club for townsfolk performances. This was followed by a stint at Marlow, and we finished the tour in Kingston. Although we had good audiences throughout the summer we were still very short of money and depended on the rent from our lodgers.

García Lorca (killed August 19, 1936, aged 38)

Following the end of our 1985 season at Kingston, we moved the barge to Richmond, where some puppeteer friends of ours, operating as the London Puppet Players, gave a season. The players were Susanne Forster, Stefan Fichert and George Speaight. Both Susanne and Stefan had worked at the Little Angel Theatre with Juliet, and George, who had helped us with our first journey to Pitstone, was a well-known puppet historian and model theatre enthusiast.

It was George who introduced us to both Richmond and Bamber Gascoigne. Bamber, a celebrity at that time, hosted *University Challenge*, a long-running television show. George wrote to us:

The Port of London Authority has now given permission to moor the Puppet Theatre Barge at Richmond between September 3 and 8. Bamber Gascoigne is willing to provide electric power from his boathouse on the riverside. Could we have an early meeting to survey the site and discuss the various problems that arise?

We were able to moor the barge below St Helena Terrace where Bamber lived and, as promised, he allowed us to draw power from his boathouse socket. We were totally unaware of the effect of high or low tide on the barge mooring at Richmond until Bamber informed us; even then, we naively left the problem of coping with the different water levels to Stefan, who was staying on board. Although we had had one scare with the tide, when we had just left the boatyard at the city end of the Thames, our turn with tidal dangers and problems between Richmond and Brentford was to come and haunt us.

We later discovered that Bamber would swim upstream with the incoming tide as far as Teddington, turn around as the tide turned, and swim back to Richmond, the outgoing tide carrying him at full speed.

Bamber Gascoigne at the time

When the Puppet Players' season ended we moved back to Camden once more, not knowing what was in store for us but hoping for the best.

Chapter 12

Experience

All experience is an arch to build upon.
Henry Brooks Adams
The Education of Henry Adams (1907)

In Camden we had to dance around the power arrangements, and at one time we even ran a telephone extension under the water across the canal. This was done secretly as it would have been frowned on by everyone. It is lucky that a passing propeller didn't chop it up. Needless to say, once our mobile phone began to be more reliable we were able to do away with the landline altogether.

We opened the autumn 1985 season with *Thomas the Rhymer,* a show based on an anonymous poem called *True Thomas*. It was published in a delightful collection entitled *Other Men's Flowers*, put together by one Field Marshal A P Wavell, whose awards were G.C.B., G.C.S.I., G.C.I.E., C.M.G., M.C., KStJ and PC. (What these stand for is a mystery.) The epigram on the title page is worth quoting:

I have gathered a posy of other men's flowers
And nothing but the thread that binds them is my own
MONTAIGNE

The adaptation was a short half-hour piece supported by a new version of *Monkey Business*, this time called *Monkey Tricks* – the show changed titles a number of times as we added new tricks and turns. During the same season, we also presented *The Butterfly's Spell*; the music for this, and for *Thomas*, was composed by Rory Allam. Sadly Rory, who composed a few

69

scores for our productions, was struck down with multiple sclerosis; he finally passed away while still a young man and we miss him greatly. He lives on in his music, which is still used in our productions today.

Theatre under construction c.1981; part of the roof raised on hinged sides in ice and snow

As Christmas approached, the weather began to get colder and continued to do so. We battled to keep warm with our coal stoves at each end of the barge, lighting the fires with an old-fashioned brass paraffin blowtorch. Finally, the snow melted, and the season ran on until the end of April, when we escaped to Little Venice for the Inland Waterways Association's Canalway Cavalcade.

The summer had been planned out in fine detail, taking in four festivals as well as two additional mooring stops. We approached the tour with some trepidation, largely owing to the huge effort required to raise and lower the roof every time we moored up and again when we upped anchor and made for the next location. The thought of doing this twelve times was enough to cause many a nightmare!

When we originally converted the barge into a puppet theatre, we realised that we needed to increase the height inside in order to have raked seating and present long-string marionettes. We designed a system that allowed side panels, which supported the roof, to be raised or lowered; this meant the roof could be at a higher level during performances, when the barge was moored up, and at a lower level while it was travelling.

When we first started using this system we worked by hand; it was a very big endeavour. The roof of the barge is made up of hatch boards; each one in heavy ply, measuring roughly 5ft by 4ft. We had to take off all the boards individually, lift off the heavy steel transom bars that held the boards in place, then fold down the side panels, which were hinged to the sides of the barge. We then placed the transom bars back at a lower level, and replaced the boards to form the roof. Finally, the order came to "sheet up", which is barge-speak for putting on the canvas and wedging it in. When all was shipshape we were ready to sail; it was a long process.

We improved this process after a few years; with borrowed money we modified the roof into one piece, so we could raise and lower it with four chain hoists. This new system has saved us a lot of trouble and labour. Now, when we are going to travel after a season of shows, we raise the roof on the hoists a couple of inches above the sides, which are then folded down into the barge before the whole roof lowers down into the original position. After sheeting up again the barge is ready to go. Still hard work, but much easier than it once was.

In this picture, the sides can be seen hinged down inside the barge, with the hoists supporting the roof. Each of the four hoists is manned when lowering or raising the roof. Juliet is smiling because it is so much easier to operate than the old system.

After a short stay in Little Venice we were off once more on our summer tour. Our first stop, and our first festival, was at Kingston. The experience there turned out to be radical, owing to a decision made by the local authority.

After Kingston Council became aware of our presence at the festival, an environmental officer paid a visit to make an inspection. He thought we might need an entertainment licence. Gren explained that, before setting up the barge, he had made an enquiry with the London County Council – the LCC, as it was known at the time – and that the person dealing with licensing theatres had told him that he did not need one. He also told the inspector that when Cromwell banned theatre he did not ban puppet theatre. We don't think he thought that a relevant factor, so he said he would return after reporting back to the council office.

The following morning, just prior to the opening of the festival, the officer returned. He said the five Kingston officers had discussed the issue and three of the five decided that, as we did not assume a role or play live music, we did not need a licence. Following that decision, we always quoted this ruling when confronted by an authority, as it is stated in the Theatres Act of 1968.

> " play " means—
>   (a) any dramatic piece, whether involving improvisation or not, which is given wholly or in part by one or more persons actually present and performing and in which the whole or a major proportion of what is done by the person or persons performing, whether by way of speech, singing or action, involves the playing of a role ; and
>   (b) any ballet given wholly or in part by one or more persons actually present and performing, whether or not it falls within paragraph (a) of this definition ;

As soon as the festival was over we packed up, took down the roof and started the engine, making for Chertsey and our second festival, which was due to open in a week. The run from Kingston to Chertsey is not long and we were making that journey for the second time in the barge's history. We soon put the roof up and did our bit – then roof down again and ready for the long run to Sandford Lock, near Oxford. Our two weeks there went by so fast we had hardly raised the roof when we had to take it down again and head off for the Henley Festival.

Once more we enjoyed the glamour and excitement of Henley and then the roof came down and we were off to Marlow for a week's shows, topped and tailed by two weekends, before we had to take the roof down yet again and face a monumental journey. This time we were travelling all the way to the Royal Festival Pier to start a season for Summer Scope, a South Bank festival to which we had been invited by the Festival Hall management. The festival boss was Simon Rattle, the young conductor who was to become world famous. He had come to see *Thomas the Rhymer* earlier in the year, when we were in Camden, and approved of Rory's music – it was that, we think, that got us the job.

Tucked in on the South Bank

Docking at the Festival Pier was fraught with danger and stress. Fortunately, we had engaged a tug to take us downriver and guide us, which turned out to be a very wise move. By the time we passed Westminster Abbey the tide was really moving fast, going out, so we tied a rope between the tug and the barge so that the tug man could hold us steady with his strong tug engine. It was very tricky getting onto the pier. Sue and our daughter Kate were with us at the time and they had to leap off the moving barge and get a rope onto the pier bollard, in seconds, so we could avoid a head-on crash into the pier walkway. By coincidence Paul Deverell, who had helped us in the early days of the barge, happened to be on the pier and was heard shouting humorous insults such as, "There's always trouble when you're around!"

The experience on the river and the long run of shows for the South Bank festival was a great adventure. Friends and relatives visited, and it was a case of party-party from August 4 to 31 – with a few hangovers. One morning Gren was complaining about his hangover to a ticket tout on the bank who replied, "Don't worry mate – one day you will wake up and you will be in bed with a seventy-year-old". Gren didn't believe him!

Following the festival, we set off on our own to Limehouse Dock, moving downstream on a very big Thames where the other craft around us looked enormous and the barge felt tiny and insignificant. Our timing around the tide movement was quite good but the water filter got clogged up with floating flotsam , causing us some stress. Nonetheless, we made it safely into Limehouse and from there onto the canal and back to Camden.

Entering Limehouse Lock

Chapter 13

Licence to Play

Law is a bottomless pit.
Dr Arbuthnot
The History of John Bull (1712)

The mooring on the main canal in Camden was, as before, unsatisfactory, and now it was worse because we lost our power source. The lock cottage where we had been plugged in was being altered for letting out. We managed, with due permissions, to solve the problem by hiring the builder on the cottage job to dig a trench running from the gate at Chalk Farm Road to the barge mooring. It was about 300 feet long, so this was no mean feat. We had a power source installed by the London Electricity Board, known as LEB, at the gate position, and from there we ran a cable to the barge. Although the cost of the facility meant more debt, it was worth it at the time. There was no alternative.

Unfortunately, our position parallel to the wall forced us to have our gangplank running up onto the front of the barge, with no direct access to the land from the second exit on the side of barge. This was not ideal and led to a confrontation with a schoolteacher.

A school had booked three performances on the barge. At the first show a teacher complained about the health and safety aspects, and in particular the emergency exits. They then went back to the school and reported the inadequate fire escape; the head teacher cancelled the next two performances. Juliet insisted they paid for the cancelled shows and subsequently the head called in the authorities.

So down came the fire department in the form of an ugly man, a nasty piece of work. He had a gleaming face, closely shaved apart from a thin line of a moustache, just above his top lip, leaving shiny skin between the moustache and his nose. Needless to say, his boots were equally shiny.

He shut us down at once and gave us a list of things that needed changing or removing and left saying he would be back. Gren worked like a madman through the night removing all the oil lamps to which the inspector had objected and installing some of those extension lights that are used for car repairs, which he hung in strategic places. Fortunately, we had an old emergency exit light given to us by our friend Dana Norgren who had owned a restaurant and had no further use for it, so we also installed that. This new lighting changed the scene and ambience in the barge completely, for the worse, but we did manage to improve the atmosphere later on. Finally, we moved the barge, putting it parallel to the wharf leaving the aft end sticking out under the bridge; not good for security, but good for the audience access and fire exit.

The next day a more senior fire department man came to inspect. He was much more reasonable, and said, "OK, that's fine, no problem". Whereupon we reopened. His ruling did not last long, however, as after a few days the original man, who was his junior, visited once more and just wasn't having it. So, he shut us down again and informed the Inner London Education Authority (ILEA). That really damaged our reputation, for a while.

This was followed by a visit from a Health and Safety Inspector of Factories, a Mr Clubley. One of a number of inspectors who cover the country, he was very helpful. Basically, all premises used by the public fall into their remit, not just factories. They are very highly trained, and their job is to bridge the divide that exists between business owners and the fire department or any other civil authorities that may have a complaint. In our case he organised a meeting with the fire department and our engineer, on site at the barge. We were all there together on the wharf deciding what had to be done. Mr Clubley's ruling would be final, which was a great help because the fire department can change the goalposts any time. Sadly, our problems were not over and worse was to follow. After the work on the barge had been completed, as agreed at the meeting, the fire department neglected to lift their ban. Primarily this affected school bookings.

But luck was on our side once more in the form of a friend, Kay Davenport, an American from Dallas and the partner of an artist who Gren had known from his South African days. Kay is an Oxford intellectual, very clever and as tough as any Texan. Her brothers, successful lawyers, had suggested to her that she undertake a law course (which takes a year or two if you have a degree already) as then she would always be able to get a job. She had completed a doctorate at Oxford and was just about to qualify as a lawyer.

We explained to Kay how the fire department had put the closure on us and that, after we had completed the required alterations they had not informed the authorities, in particular the ILEA, leaving us in limbo and losing work. Kay wrote to the fire department and told them to inform the ILEA that we were fully operational and offering school performances, with their approval. If they did not do so she would sue immediately. It was just amazing; they acted within hours of receiving her letter. So, we got back on an even keel and started working with schools again. The loss of revenue didn't seem to be important at that time because we were poor anyway and when you're poor, you're poor. End of story.

We have had quite a few such things happen over the years, with the authorities coming at us wanting to intimidate and threaten to close the theatre down. Some individuals love to threaten. The way they act when they've got a bit of power is totally revolting, like abusive bullies who really want to beat you up. We should add that not everyone is like that!

It takes a long time to gain the trust of the authorities and build an audience. Little adventures happen all the time and in between, a reputation, one way or the other, is gained.

At the time there was quite a lot of truancy on the local estates and often young boys would come down to Camden Lock and knock the hell out of whatever they could lay their hands on. One year the canal had frozen and someone had thrown our A-board onto the ice. (The A-board was used to chalk up the times and shows that were currently being performed.) Gren was busy trying to retrieve the board with a boat hook, which was slightly short, putting the board out of reach. He was leaning over the edge of the wharf trying to hook it when he fell, plonk, straight through the ice. Juliet, who was below deck, heard the terrible crash and knew what had happened. Out she came from the barge and there was

Kate, Juliet and Gren at Camden, 1987

nothing to be seen, just a hole in the ice! Gren had disappeared. Fortunately, he had learned about water and was a good swimmer. He explained later that if you have swum as a youth, as he had, you get to understand what happens underwater. After crashing through the ice he immediately looked up and could see the light patch, so he knew where the hole was and went shooting up; out he came with overcoat and boots still on! Juliet pulled him out and then phoned an old school friend who lived in Camden asking for help. Her partner came and picked Gren up in his car and took him to their house, put him in the bath and gave him a brandy. He soon recovered, dressed himself in borrowed clothes and went back to the barge to do the show.

Traumatic events like this were happening all the time. We do remember one funny moment, although it did not seem funny at the time. Some young scallywags had been causing trouble and doing various naughty things about the place, so one day Gren followed them to see where they went. He followed them for a long way, along the canal and into a local estate, before eventually losing them. Towards the end they became aware of him. They knew where he had come from and Gren could see that they were beginning to get paranoid. That evening we were on the barge when they appeared on the curved bridge at Camden Lock, and started shouting and swearing at us, "… come out you effing bloody coward …", and the like. They wouldn't or couldn't let go. So then Gren, thinking it was quite humorous, put a white hanky on a pole and stuck it out of the porthole of the barge, indicating he wanted a truce. A couple of the boys cottoned on, but the majority, about twenty of them, who ranged between the ages of eight and fourteen, continued to taunt us.

The flag of peace didn't work. So Gren thought to himself that he would have to face the music. Juliet and a friend of hers were on the barge with Gren – no match for twenty delinquents! We knew at that moment that Gren would have to go up there. "Come on ... get out ... ya ...", they shouted.

Gren set out, and as he came off the gangplank they spat at him. Gren takes up the story:

"I continued on under the curved bridge and wiped all the spit off, then carried on walking around the corner and up to the foot of the bridge to face them. I approached slowly but deliberately, walking towards them as they stood there, standing dead still and silent; then suddenly, at the last minute, they turned and ran like a flock of birds. Their last aggressive action was to throw the A-board into the canal once more. I never saw them again, after that. Perhaps they thought they had had the last word."

Later on, we moved to Little Venice, Paddington, and said goodbye to Camden forever. It is a nostalgic memory, but all things change all the time and the move was for the better.

Eleven groups of people: *a painting of Camden Lock by Nick Herbert*

Chapter 14

New Water

How far that little candle throws his beams!
So shines a good deed in a naughty world.
William Shakespeare
The Merchant of Venice, Act 5, Scene 1

In the spring of 1988 we arrived in Little Venice, a completely different situation from the one we had been in over the past five years. The self-styled "Commandant" of Browning's Pool was Mr Alex Prowse, a watercolourist with two narrow boats. The first was a gallery and the second served as living accommodation. He later changed these for two wide barges and was our neighbour for many years. Alex had his finger in every pie and told us we were only permitted to be there because he allowed it! We answered that we knew this. He welcomed us grudgingly, unlike Tony Hopkins who ran Jason's Trip boats from a yard nearby. Tony did eventually accept our presence, however, and became friendly.

We started to recover from the traumas of Camden and slowly discovered that West London is not the same as North London. Paddington lads were tougher than their Camden counterparts, both more ruthless and sophisticated. Gren became aware of this when we were given our second welcome to Little Venice by a group of tough, delinquent-looking boys, maybe fifteen years old, hanging around the barge watching us. It was difficult to know how to deal with the situation, but after a few days of it Gren asked them to come in and see a show. He gave them some tickets and told them it was on at 3 o'clock. Two boys came back. We showed them to their seats and they sat there and watched the performance. One was the leader, the other, who looked

Browning's Pool at Little Venice, named after the poet Browning

very much more suspicious, his sidekick. The leader was sharp; he could see that Gren was showing him respect, in some kind of a way. After the show Gren asked him how he got on with it and he replied, "Oh yeah … ya know". Then off they went, and we never had any trouble in that neck of the woods again. Amazing. That was really positive; these things happen. Such is life!

Although our mooring position in the pool was much more satisfactory at Little Venice than at Camden, with far better access for the public, we were not reassured by the complete calm and tranquillity of the place, after the crowds and hustle and bustle of Camden Lock. With so little foot traffic, would we be able to pick up extra audience members? In fact, would the public come and find us in such a quiet spot? It took us several years to realise that it was the perfect place for us and the public loved to "discover" us there.

Not only was the move to Little Venice a sea change in our operation, but also in the same period we acquired an Amstrad green-screen personal computer, at a cost of £400.

Working day and night, it took us two weeks to learn how to type a sentence! After that we were well away and gave up using Tippex and

The Amstrad with printer

taking twenty to thirty minutes to type a letter. After about eighteen months of using the Amstrad we graduated to a Windows PC and since that time we have gone even further and become Apple snobs.

As for our sound equipment, used both for recording and for playback on the barge, we graduated from a Revox quarter-inch tape to a four-track TASCAM. CD was followed by MiniDisc before everything turned totally digital. Now sound recording and editing is all done using computers and digital recorders, and playback is through a computer.

It wasn't long after we had mastered the Amstrad that we were introduced to Adam Brett, a Cambridge friend of Rob Humphreys, our daughter Kate's partner. Adam came and worked for us, part time; he introduced us to Westminster Arts Council and taught us the rudiments of Microsoft Windows.

Having got settled in at Little Venice, we had the time and energy to think more carefully about future projects locally and how our work might develop in the area.

Our touring life seemed to take care of itself, with invitations arriving to attend festivals abroad in exotic places. Home was a different matter. Adam had made contact with Westminster Arts Council, members of which duly came to see the theatre and attend a show. We subsequently managed to arrange a meeting with Margaret Leask, who was chief arts officer at the time. She suggested we should design a school's workshop for Key Stages 1 and 2 using shadow puppets. She also gave us some good advice on costing and wages for puppeteers, on the understanding that if we put in a satisfactory application, Westminster Arts would consider supporting such a project. This led to 25 years of continuous support for our educational work in the borough. The workshops were facilitated by Kate and Natasha, both of whom helped design and foster them from the start. Juliet recalls the early days:

"We decided early on in the planning that we did not want to go into schools just to demonstrate and then make shadow puppets, but rather that we wanted to offer the pupils an opportunity to create their own characters and actually construct them themselves, with our help, which could lead to them putting on short plays of their own.

Pupils making shadow puppets

With this in mind, I realised that we were making our lives difficult in more ways than one. First of all, we would need to allow a full day for the children to understand the nature of shadow theatre, learn how to produce an image on the screen with light, and then to make a shadow puppet of their own – let alone to put on a short show. So now we were asking for a full day out of the busy curriculum, which at a time when SATS were already taking a grip on the school day, was a big ask. We also required a big space for screens and lighting and, most presumptuous of all, a total or partial blackout! What a hope. However, on the plus side we could offer the workshops at a generously subsidised rate if Westminster awarded us the funding, while another excellent incentive was the connection to the Key Stages 1 and 2 curriculum, which we studied carefully. The English, Design and Technology and Science modules were perfect for us to key into, with the potential to demonstrate storytelling, design, light and shade, use of tools and so on. These gave us just the selling points we needed.

So, we researched, prepared, designed and finally put in an application to Westminster, having approached forty primary schools in the borough and received around 25 positive replies. We hoped for support and we did get it. Suddenly everything became a reality and we were flat out building shadow screens, buying materials, planning dates, negotiating with school secretaries and talking to class teachers. The series was up and running. We tried to plan the dates consecutively, so that the puppeteers could have a block of work over several weeks. Natasha and Kate were the main facilitators, with Rachel Leonard who had trained with us and, later, Colleen Magennis, who would travel down from the Isle of Bute to take part. I met Colleen in Little Angel days and we have remained friends ever since. She is an imaginative, independent and talented artist who first trained as a jewellery designer and maker and followed it up with puppetry. Now we have regular collaborations on Movingstage projects, when she will come and design and build with us for several weeks. It is always exciting, a pleasure and fun. It doesn't feel like work. With this strong team, we proceeded to run the shadow puppet workshops for many years."

Behind the scenes at a school workshop

Natasha and Kate went on to other things and different puppeteers facilitated. We had some wonderful feedback from class teachers that made us feel very proud, and we knew that the difficulties encountered in running the full-day workshop, with everything that it entailed, were worth it. A fairly frequent response from teachers was astonishment at seeing a quiet or non-participatory child lose his or her inhibitions and come to life verbally and manually with a puppet.

The characters invented by the children were sometimes memorable. When we started the workshops, it was the era of the Spice Girls, so there were plenty of them, along with princesses, while the boys made football heroes. One unforgettable effort was declared to be Elvis Presley on the *Titanic*. The children's

Children present a show as others watch

favourite part was presenting their own shows. We put them in groups of five or six and each group performed while the rest of the class watched, so they learned how to be an audience too. This could be bedlam at the end of the day, but we all enjoyed it and it was often very funny. Most class teachers got into the spirit of the day but occasionally we had to coax them along, especially if they were unprepared.

As well as supporting our work in schools, Westminster Arts Council guaranteed our winter seasons at Little Venice. This allowed us to continue developing new work and also to pay our puppeteers properly, knowing that we would not make a loss. Up to this time both of us had operated all the shows – other than the adult productions – without help. Now we could engage a puppeteer to work with us on the family shows, which also allowed us to make improvements.

At this time, we were often asked to take a touring show into small venues, arts centres and schools. Touring marionettes with our steel stage was not a practical option for these bookings and we concluded that something else was required. The answer was a shift to rod-puppet production with a lightweight stage. We could use this for touring small-scale venues, private parties and schools. And so began a new phase. Some might call it progress.

We set about the project with vigour. Juliet made the puppets, from wood and sculpted foam, and Gren built a wooden touring stage. We had a work placement at the time, Charlotte Dore, who helped with the construction of the puppet booth. Charlotte went on to live in the USA and now runs her own puppet company.

Juliet's puppets are operated and supported by a central rod attached to the head and a shorter rod to the body; there are also detachable hand rods. The puppets are light and strong and easier to manage than marionettes. Research shows that this type of puppet arrived in England no earlier than the 1930s. The booth is also lightweight and easy to put up. The show requires two operators and sound playback equipment. Since that first booth and show we have gone on to make two more rod-puppet shows, plus a more sophisticated booth.

The touring aspect worked out well and added good income to the company coffers. Kate and Natasha worked tirelessly, with other puppeteers, taking the new set-up to schools, village halls, festivals and events all over the country.

Sadly, in 2009, our school support from Westminster ended. Cuts were biting, and in 2012 the support for the winter season stopped. It was a blow at the time, but we knew it was going to happen as there had been a change of policy for Westminster arts funding.

By then our publicity was on a much stronger footing, being driven by the internet. The barge website had been up and running since the end of the nineties, which gave us access to a far wider public. This was followed by online booking and everything that social media could offer. Now we take bookings from every part of the globe and are no longer dependent on postal mail-outs or distribution of printed material. The internet is without doubt a fantastic, and inexpensive, tool for publicity and exposure for a small organisation like ours. It would be correct to say that now, at the time of writing, houses are more often full than not. In the early days we did well considering we were launching something new, small and unusual with virtually no capital, but at that time digital equipment, Xboxes, games, smartphones and tablets with every sort of entertainment on them did not exist. Competition was less, and parents brought along children of up to ten or eleven years old. Now this age group is less likely to come and there is a trend for more adults to attend without children. Students in pairs or groups of adult tourists now book frequently.

Chapter 15

New Ground

Poetry is a subject as precise as geometry.
Gustave Flaubert
Letter to Louise Colet (August 14, 1853)

Like all the seasons in England, after the winter of 1988 the English spring was bursting out all over, as was Gren's idea for a new original production. He takes over the story:

"I had been to see our daughter Louise perform in the play *Tom and Viv*, by Michael Hastings, and fallen in love with Vivienne, who was called the 'River Girl' when she was a young single woman. T S Eliot had fallen for and subsequently married her, which was her downfall. It is a tragic story.

Isis looking upstream

Meanwhile, the central arch of Henley Bridge carries two stone carvings; on the one side, looking towards the sea, is the head of Father Thames and on the other side is the head of Isis, looking towards the River Isis that feeds into the Thames with fresh water.

I had reflected on those carvings depicted on the bridge for four years and now, having seen the play, in which my daughter movingly acted out the tragedy of Vivienne Haigh-Wood, I conceived an idea for a marionette play and set about finding a writer for the project.

On May 23, 1988, I wrote to Michael Hastings, complimenting him on his play and enclosing my synopsis for a marionette production, asking him if he would be interested in writing a new play based on it. I thought it the proper thing to do, as his original work was the main source for the idea. He rejected it on the grounds that 'your own style of inventiveness for a moving travelling show would be best for the project'.

The River Girl, Poet and Cronies

Michael had no idea about or knowledge of marionette drama – not many people have. I wasn't surprised, and fortunately I already had a poet in mind. If words are an integral part of a production, it is my contention that poetic writing is the best form for marionette drama. I set about contacting Wendy Cope, whose poetry is both pithy and humorous. It was wonderful when she agreed to write a verse drama from my plot and subsequently she sent us some 135 stanzas. I had to look up what a 'stanza' was and discovered that it is 'an arrangement of a certain number of lines, usually four or more, sometimes having a fixed length, meter, or rhyme scheme, forming a division of a poem'.

However, Wendy needed time to develop the play and we were happy to agree to an eight- to twelve-month period in which she could do this. This gave us time to attend to another exciting project which presented itself to us unexpectedly."

A young man, Harry Marshall, working as a television researcher, came to see a show on the barge and stayed for a chat afterwards; he was keen to get a TV project about our work off the ground. Although the project did not materialise, we discovered during the process that Harry had written a narrative poem about a baboon who wanted to fly to the moon!

The Babuscha Baboon woke up one night
And saw that the moon was full.
Such a beautiful moon there never had been
"I shall fly there with a balloon!" She cried
"I shall fly there with a balloon!"

She wasted no time and with creepers and vine
And the help of the weaver birds
A basket she wove in that moonlit grove,
A basket to fly to the moon high above,
All to fly to the silvery moon.

Baboon and Monkey

This was right up our street. Juliet immediately asked Harry if we could see a copy and then asked for permission to make a production of the poem. He agreed, so we set about making the puppets and designing the scenery. It turned out to be a real success and is now in our regular repertoire. The first performance was on the river at Sandford, at the beginning of the 1988 summer tour.

Harry sent us a postcard after seeing the show, which we read with all nerves tingling

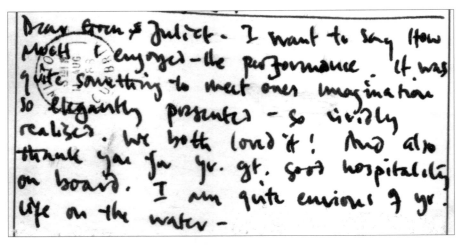

An excerpt from Harry's card

The summer tour continued as we progressed downriver and soon the Christmas season had come and gone. From the moment Wendy agreed to write her poem, *The River Girl*, we started planning and designing the production and then making the puppets. We received the final draft on March 19, 1989, and set about arranging the recording of the voices and commissioning Rory Allam to write the music. Our two main actors were John Hodgkinson and our daughter Louise.

The marionette construction was influenced by a puppet that John Roberts had lent us. John is a well-known maker and excellent carver. The look of the puppets grew out of the two Henley bridge carvings. The figure of Isis was tricky to design as she had to swim gracefully under water and walk on land. As the making was completed, Juliet set about stringing and costuming the characters one by one.

Father Thames

At Henley Festival on Saturday July 5, 1989, at 7.30pm *The River Girl* was performed for the first time and broke new ground in marionette drama. This was an out-of-London run before the official opening, planned for when we had finished the tour. We calculated it would be well 'run in' by then. This exciting evening was also the 150th anniversary of the Henley Regatta – a double whammy of celebration. In addition to Henley we presented seasons at both Marlow and Richmond, with a visit from Wendy at Marlow.Following the Richmond season, we made our way back to Little Venice and were happy to find our mooring intact with no awful order to move anywhere else. We opened the winter season with a production incorporating some of Aesop's fables.

The Hare challenges the Tortoise

The show ran from the beginning of November to the end of February with full houses at practically every performance. We then went on to present our good old standby, the double bill *The Birdman* and *Monkey Business*.

On May 9, 1990, we finally staged the London opening of *The River Girl*. The illustrious audience included Wendy and ten guests; John Hodgkinson and Louise; Rory Allam, the composer; Kenneth Griffith, the actor who voiced many of our productions; Christopher Leith, puppeteer; and Helen Rose, the *Time Out* drama critic, along with many friends and family.

The following review, by Helen Rose, appeared in *Time Out*:

A young man sits gazing at the silvery-green rippling flow of the Thames. He is a poet with writer's block, a man without rhyme, until the River Girl, Princess Isis, breaks the surface and smilingly gives him the words and dreams of which verses are made. Such is their love that she leaves her river home and they marry. He prospers, becomes famous, starts boozing and neglects his beautiful muse. Wendy Cope's poem, commissioned by the Movingstage Marionette Co, has the quirky grace and neatly fashioned detail of the puppet for whom she is writing. There is an ironic bite to Ms Cope's exposure of the vagaries of literary fame and a wicked delight in her subtle poetic mud-slinging at the profession in general, but she has a delicate, romantic touch too which is movingly animated in the puppets' gestures. As always, one's imagination is captured by the skilful manipulation as they miraculously embrace and kiss without tangling the wires which bring them so realistically to life.

The poetic play was later broadcast on BBC Radio 3 and the poem was published by Faber & Faber. Wendy very kindly acknowledges us both for the original idea. All in all the *River Girl* episode was a most wonderful experience and taught us both an enormous amount. The consequent London season of the production was an uphill struggle as it was very difficult in the eighties and nineties to get an adult audience for a grown-up production. However, we kept going with adult productions and soon we were to commission another contemporary writer.

Little Venice, always beautiful, was the ideal spot to open *The River Girl*. It is a pearl of a place to have a mooring and we have been lucky to have been there for more than three decades. Unlike Camden Lock, Little Venice just doesn't change. New brooms appear every few years with new ideas, but fortunately they can't sweep anything away. Quite often a bright spark will arrive wanting to sell liquor from a tarty boat, but there is a powerful residency around the pool which soon puts a stop to such terrible ideas.

The River Girl carved by Gren

Chapter 16

Summer Holiday

On every formal visit a child ought to be of the party,
by way of provision for discourse.

Jane Austen

Sense and Sensibility (1811)

Winter is always quite tough on the barge, so we tend to keep away as much as possible between performances and get on with admin or making puppets in the workshop. After the years of taking the barge up and down the canal, followed by the journeys up the Thames, we finally realised that we needed a second vessel to accommodate the domestic side of life. At various points in the early years, while in Adelaide Dock having work done on the barge, we noticed a slightly smaller barge moored there. It belonged to canal man Gerry Heward, who had been living on it. Because of the excellent winch on the front of the boat, which he craved for the puppet barge, Gren made overtures to Gerry and the long and short of it is that we bought it from him and slowly converted it. This would not have been possible without help from Val Humphreys, Rob's mother. Kate and Rob had been together for a while and Val decided to come in as joint owner of our new boat, which allowed us to survey, repair and install an engine in her. *Eroda* is an old barge built in Hull around 1920, originally used as a weed cutter on the Norfolk Broads. Around 60 feet long with a beam of about 10 foot, she is an elegant shape, fine on river or canal. Since being converted, she has accompanied the barge and served the company well, both for accommodation and as a backup for towing the puppet barge when it broke down. This was important, as it meant that we could always get to the designated mooring in time for any scheduled performance. In fact, we have never missed a performance in 35 years. We managed well as co-owners, as expenses were shared and Val was able to enjoy some leisure time on board over the years while we were touring the Thames.

On board Eroda – Middletons and Pitt-Doyles: Stan, Joshua, Kate, Ben, Jan, Jasmine

Gren writes:

"Spring 1990 was a sunny welcome into the next decade. We were beginning to get control of our finances. I had managed to secure three mooring spaces at King's Cross, on a lease from the former Railways Property Board, which I was able to let out. This brought in an income that helped subsidise the Puppet Barge and proved an asset for a number of years. Later we managed to obtain permission to have more boats there, whereupon I bought three wooden pontoons from Chichester Harbour and had them delivered and lowered into the canal at Goodsway. More mooring fees soon made loan payments easier and we were able to consider the next commission."

Our Kate had been working as a stage manager and had a job on a production called *The Bite of the Night*, written by Howard Barker. She let us know that it was interesting writing. Having got to know Barker's work, we thought he would be a good man to write an original play for us. But in the meantime we had to prepare for the summer tour, which was fast approaching, before we could consider these ambitious thoughts.

As we were presenting past productions, we did not have to think about new staging, and the tour was becoming routine. This time *Sir Gawain* was the fare, alongside *The Hare and the Tortoise and other Tales from Aesop* (a new title for an old show). Both productions are suitable for all ages: the first is good for grown-ups and slightly older children, the second for everyone, and both fitted Jane Austen's dictum. We had come a long way since the Andy Farquharson days and it was an enjoyable summer, for a change.

The tour started in June at Wallingford, a new mooring position. We were moored up on the towpath and drew power from someone's barn. Memory is a bit thin, but opposite our mooring was a park that served as a gathering place for the local youth – not a pretty noise, or sight for that matter. The town centre was neat and tidy, but the place itself was generally dull – that said, we attracted good audiences.

Back: Dave Schaal, Rob Humphreys, Simon Oatley, Andy Doyle
Front: Lesley Muggeridge, Katerine Poupart, Michel Monte, Brigitte Poupart, Gren, Louise

After Wallingford we went on to Henley, followed by Marlow and Richmond, with wonderful full houses all the way. This helped enormously towards keeping the bank loan in trim. Fortunately, we didn't have to pay wages as we both did the operating and the trainee worked as front of house manager. Looking back on those times it is difficult to imagine how we managed. We did, of course, have our family and friends to help us, especially when putting the roof up and down. Featured here is a snapshot taken by Juliet of a typical group of friends gathered together after Henley Festival had finished. Following the merriment, the work of moving the barge up to the Leander Club mooring would proceed with the help of these friends.

The summer months were, and are still, a good time for plotting what to do next. After beating a path up and down the Thames for six years, we had almost finished our apprenticeship on two counts: the first on the running of the barge as a public venue, and the second on navigating the river. Both still present problems from time to time. Management of the public is an art in itself, as there is such a diversity of folk who come to the performances and now and then problems arise and have to be handled. Also, everything that is brought onto a boat has to be taken off, the worst of which is the waste. The barge has a large holding tank that has to be pumped out and the timing of the pump-out is crucial because there are not many pump-out stations. Sometimes a big tanker lorry known as the "lavender truck" has to be booked, which is expensive. We could cope with this by now!

Knowing how to handle these issues, we had a relaxed summer, which was a refreshing change after the past few years. Planning and plotting was easier and much more fun, which made the prospect of the forthcoming decade more enjoyable. Fate was to play a few nasty cards, but thank goodness we could not see into the future.

When a person learns to ride a bicycle, the pain and struggle is enormous. There is a point, a very microsecond in the eternity of time, when the discipline is mastered. When this happens the know-how of balancing on two wheels becomes part of the instinct. This phenomenon may also be experienced when a person learns to handle a marionette or a barge.

Gren continues:

"As a young assistant cameraman, I was working on a film for the South African Tourist Corporation, known as SATOUR. This semi-governmental unit produced high-quality documentaries for screening in Europe and America in order to promote South African tourism. At the time, we were filming a marionette show, being performed by the John Wright company. John subsequently started the Little Angel Theatre in London. This was long before I came to England and before I had any notion of puppetry. In fact, it was the first time I had seen a puppet show, let alone a puppet. I was about 21 years old at the time.

That very first moment of witnessing a marionette show was the start of an illusion. The fact that I was drawn into the marionette world twenty years after the filming experience was part of the same illusion. Webster tells me that an illusion is an unreal image presented to the bodily or mental vision; a deceptive appearance; a false show or hallucination. I realise now, in retrospect, that the thought of making a marionette show with my partner was an illusion and that the proposed construction of a puppet theatre on a barge was also an illusion, brought about by the earlier experience. The point is that the making of a puppet show and the puppet theatre on a barge was one *big* illusion. More than three thousand years ago Aristotle said, 'Probable impossibilities are to be preferred to improbable possibilities.'

Had the planning and making of a marionette drama as well as the construction of a puppet theatre on a barge been approached from what some might call the *realistic* point of view, the theatre would never have been made. And, be under no illusion, it would be impossible and sheer madness to attempt the same project in this day and age, because of the changes in monetary value, law, and health and safety regulations. Expenses are higher now, and it was easier to manipulate one's money in the past. But, who knows? Someone, somewhere in the world is bound to be suffering from a big illusion."

1990 was a year of philosophic thinking and regeneration of the spirit, made better by the fact that we returned from the river once more and were greeted by our own mooring in Little Venice. To this day, canal users will tell you how precious and valuable a decent mooring is. As we write this, the Canal and River Trust has renewed our mooring licence. The trust surveyor, Mr Martin Hime, was fair and an absolute gentleman when the negotiations took place. In fact, over the past three decades there have been only three or perhaps four bad apples in the canal barrel. Sadly, however, Martin Hime has moved on and no longer works for the Trust.

Chapter 17

Questions

Unless we change direction, we are likely
to end up where we are headed.
Chinese proverb

As the winter of 1990 progressed, new ideas were forming in regard to our ambitions. One of them was to make a big production that we could tour nationally. Gren asked the question: what exactly is a puppet show? Traditionally it is one thing, but in these changing times it can be quite another experience. There have been vast positive technological changes, but also today humans are appearing with puppets, destroying the illusion traditionally offered by a puppet show. Some of those guilty are actors, turning the art form in all sorts of directions while they dominate the puppets and claim centre stage.

The questions: What is a pure form of puppetry? Should the puppet be the only protagonist? Should the human form intrude? The power of puppetry comes from the puppets, which are able to do things that the actor or animal cannot do. A pig cannot fly except as a marionette. We have opted, primarily, for long-string marionettes, without the operators in view, and that is our art. There are many arguments to be had, but in the end, as the great theorist Gordon Craig asserted, the actor's theatre cannot be a fine art because the humans who play the parts will age and therefore change – which is not the case with a puppet. Of course, the manipulator will change, but at least the art itself is close to fine art, and closer than the actor's theatre.

All through these barge years we were also touring on land, and had a number of memorable dates. One was with the Ellen Terry Barn Theatre at Smallhythe in Kent. Terry was Gordon Craig's mother. After her death, her daughter, who had been living with her, converted her barn into a theatre. Subsequently the house and barn were acquired by the National Trust which turned the house into a museum. It was a great honour to perform at the theatre. The theatre caretakers knew Teddy Craig, Gordon's son, who lived near Henley. We were able to visit Teddy and have an interesting afternoon learning about his upbringing and his relationship with his father. At the end of the day, Teddy gave us a suitcase full of puppets and ephemera that had belonged to his father. We now feel very close to Craig's theatre history and theory.

Stan starts his barge training

With the birth of Stanley, our first grandchild, and our ten years of barge experience, our apprenticeship was complete; we had to face the fact that we were grown-ups!

The thought of adulthood gave us courage to tackle our next big project: commissioning Howard Barker to write a script for us. We set about it and made contact with Howard who looked positively on the thought of a marionette drama and told us he had an idea that might work. We then had to negotiate a fee with his agent, which was a new experience, but the contract was soon drawn up and we waited, with bated breath, for the script to arrive.

While waiting, we produced a broadsheet, *The Manipulator*, using the Amstrad. It was published in March 1991 and included an essay entitled *The Spirit of the Marionette* written by John Phillips, an intellectual and a puppeteer. Then we began to design a new large touring stage, this time in aluminium. Jolyon Havinden, who had built our steel stage and was now based in Scotland, was engaged to do the job and discussions started in earnest. We were fortunate to receive a grant from the Gulbenkian Trust to finance the project. Having set the construction of the stage in motion we were ready for Barker's script.

The script duly arrived. It was an extremely complex piece of writing and was an enormous challenge to present. The title of the piece, *All He*

Fears, reflected our own fears as to how we were going to present the play. The theme deals with a philosopher who fears things so much he makes them happen. With its challenging, thoughtful dialogue, it gave us the opportunity to present a rat holding a conversation with a philosopher and other wonderful visual episodes.

In the making, we encountered a serious problem with the sound. The first recording session was ruined by a buzz on the track. The engineer and the studio were both hopeless. Barker introduced us to many talented people, one of whom was Matthew Scott, now head of music at the National Theatre, who was engaged to write the music. Matthew saved the day by introducing us to the BBC World Service in the form of Graham Harper, sound engineer and studio manager. He re-recorded the piece for us in the BBC studio. Barker wanted Ian McDiarmid to record the main part and this Ian did beautifully. Stephanie Fayerman played the rat, Harriet Walter the lover, and our daughter Louise played the prostitute.

Rat comforts Botius the Philosopher

In Scotland, the construction of the bigger, grander, aluminium touring marionette stage went ahead steadily, while in England the puppets slowly came to life. We had many more discussions with Jolyon on the phone until he delivered the stage. On setting it up, we realised that dressing it was much more work than we had imagined. It took more than a year to get all the elements made and everything assembled, but eventually we began to piece the play together and at last we were ready for rehearsal.

The bright ideas and fancy thinking that led to the commissioning and consequent making of a touring stage and new production kept us busy from 1991 through to 1993, with snatched visits to Pakistan and Palestine in the autumn of 1992. These visits were in response to invitations to perform at the first International Puppet Festival in Lahore, followed by the second International Puppet Festival in Jerusalem.

It was exactly ten years since our grand tour of Pakistan with Faizaan Peerzada in 1982, and time for another visit. Faizaan had been expanding his puppet activities and he was happy to invite us to the festival. After some debate in the family, it was proposed that Gren and Juliet would go along with Rob (Stan's father), Kate and Stan, who was now aged eighteen months and ready to start his puppet training.

From left: Kate, Stan, Rob, Karim, Juliet

We duly arrived in Islamabad and were met by Karim Khan, whom we knew well from the previous tour when he had been a great help. On this trip we were accommodated in a hotel as well as being funded by the British Council and were booked to attend the festival for two weeks.

We soon had to heave to and construct a stage. This time there were two professional carpenters and some decent timber assigned to the build, so we managed to make a fair job of the task. We had brought two shows with us: *Aesop's Fables* and a double bill comprising *The Birdman* and *Monkey Business,* which had been specifically requested as it had proved to be very popular on the previous tour. Included in the baggage, besides the puppets, were the backcloths, props and two soundtracks. Faizaan promised us a good lighting rig and sound equipment for playback.

Pakistan is a busy place. Anything that is broken is made to work, so as a result, everything works, including the people. Motorcycles are ridden four-up, holding mum, dad and the children. Buses roar up and down. Cars, scooters, rickshaws, bicycles, ox carts, horse-drawn traps, wheelbarrows and the rest are busy all day. The festival audience reflected the life and the people. This was a real festival. Candy floss and freebies, printed bags and the like; Faizaan's publicity machine saw to that. The town was covered with banners advertising the festival from one street corner to the next. Lahore is a big, ancient city; the centre of the silk route, the marketplace for the East. In Pakistan, anything that can be fabricated will be. We visited the walled inner city, passing through the ancient gates, where the atmosphere stirred one's imagination and evoked thoughts of eighteenth-century London. There were whole streets housing shops selling only silk and cotton. One lane was devoted to every kind of rope, cord and cotton on big and small reels, with string ranging from fine thread to coarse, carpet-making twine. A visit to the old mosque was an interesting experience and everyone was welcoming and friendly.

During the day we were taken to different restaurants, for lunches and dinners, in a splendidly decorated bus lined with cushioned seats and sofas for reclining on, while our hosts pointed out the city sights. Our company performed for a full week, which meant we were unable to see many of the other performances. Quick sorties into the various playing spaces were the order of the day. The festival campus was one of the best we had ever visited. The main building, known as the Arts Complex, comprised a huge circular structure with the feel of an old Roman amphitheatre. The central section housed an open-air arena capable of seating three thousand people and below this were two sophisticated theatres. The one we were playing in did not have an emergency exit, but these two venues had air conditioning, which was more than could be said for the various colourful tents around the site. The midday sun was gruelling and not even the English contingent could be seen walking about in it, although we did have our suspicions about Tim Webb of Oily Cart. He began to look more and more like a mullah as the festival continued.

We always had a packed house for the evening performances. Rob, a trained actor, would come out before the show and introduce the company, then explain briefly about Aesop and his fables, or about *Birdman* being a mime story set to music.

Kate was in charge of lighting. The board was wired up to all the spots we had rigged, but the connections often caused sparks to fly and she had quite a few shocks from the board! No health and safety requirements here, but the show went on.

Michael Meschke, the famous Swedish puppeteer, was one of the other guests performing at the festival. We knew of his work but had never met him, so it was a real treat to see his show and talk with him afterwards. He is a rare talent. He wrote of puppet manipulation, "Dexterity is a physical attribute but of not much value if it is not guided by the power to live the part".

Kate with Rob and Stan in the background

Another show we enjoyed was given by a local group of folk puppeteers. It was fast-paced and full of action, accompanied by a storyteller and musician. The staging was constructed from a traditional bed on its side with puppeteers standing behind out of view, using short string marionettes over a cloth background. There was plenty of sword fighting by warriors on camels and snake charming, among other things. After the show we spoke to the puppeteers, mostly in mime, but soon had no doubt that they were very keen for us to buy their puppets. But, we exclaimed, how can you perform if we take your puppets? They proceeded to tell us that they made new puppets all the time, in fact they had hundreds more and it was imperative that we buy them. We soon realised that this was indeed a good thing for their business and we bought a set, which hangs in the barge to this day.

The Peerzadas staged *Aladdin*, pronounced "Allah-deen", a rod show, with flourishing movement and colour. It makes a difference seeing a story that originates in the East being staged by a group from the East. The experience underlined the importance of choosing culturally compatible material for a show.

Stan's first lesson

Each evening following the puppet performances, there was a colourful extravaganza, nothing to do with puppetry, but everything to do with whirling dervishes, tribal drumming, dancing and excitement. The arena was packed with approximately three thousand spectators and at the last performance, the show drew gunfire from the security guards trying to control some over-stimulated young men.

After the gunfire died down, at the invitation of the Chief Minister of the Punjab, we were taken to a dinner in the grounds of his palace. After chicken soup, the presentation ceremony started. Each delegate was called to the podium where they were presented with a certificate and an ornate trophy. The ceremony was held outside in the palace gardens, illuminated by fairy lights. The tables, laden with delicious local dishes, were adorned with stunning ice carvings, some by Karim. The carvings melted slowly throughout the evening.

Food and music were abundant, as was the local weed that seemed to be commonplace, but there was strictly no alcohol. In fact, Faizaan carried a plastic water bottle which we later discovered contained vodka. Guests, however, were given "lite" beer and we all indulged; Rob was overcome by midnight and descended into a state of paranoia, possibly induced by the presence of armed guards, so he was pleased to get back to the hotel with Kate and Stan. However, we saw the night out and staggered home in the small hours.

The Ice Swan carved by Karim Khan

We had been in Pakistan for two weeks when the festival came to an end and it seemed that we had no sooner arrived than we had to leave; dexterity was required in counting the luggage pieces and then recounting them later before making our way to the Palestinian festival.

Boarding the train to Islamabad

Chapter 18

Travel

So it is in travelling; a man must carry knowledge with him
if he would bring home knowledge.
Samuel Johnson *(April 17, 1778) in*
James Boswell's Life of Johnson (1791)

Two days in London and then immediately to the airport, bound for
Jerusalem. Retrospectively, this arrangement must have been extremely
intense. We left Rob, Kate and Stan at home and set off with Adam
Brett who had managed to make some well-thought-out plans; but
now we can only remember our journey to Israel with loathing. We do
remember the Israeli officials at the airport searching us and our luggage
very thoroughly and questioning the motive for our visit. We discovered
that the British Council, which was funding our trip, had two offices,
one in Tel Aviv and one in East Jerusalem. This was especially confusing
as the Jerusalem office was in the Palestinian quarter, but it gave a reason
for close questioning; so close, in fact, that we had to catch a later flight.

The whole experience was very nasty and came as a big surprise owing
to our political naivety. This and our subsequent adventures taught us an
enormous amount about politics in the Middle East.

We were accommodated in a hotel that had originally been a large Arab
house. It was very comfortable, with the main rooms built around a paved
open area with tables and seating under a vine. Known, appropriately, as
the Jerusalem Hotel, it was a friendly place where we sat chatting, eating
and drinking with our hosts after shows, when time allowed. The theatre
and hotel were within walking distance of each other and were located
near the Damascus Gate, one of the many gates leading into the city. The

gate consists of one large central aperture originally intended for use by persons of high station, and two smaller side entrances for commoners. We began to realise that the Arab quarter was very different from the Jewish, Christian and Armenian quarters. The city plan is an example of sophisticated apartheid politics.

The Palestinian National Theatre is named El-Hakawati and at that time was managed by Jamal Ghosheh, a talented administrator who graduated in the UK. He was a master at raising funds from a variety of sources, ranging from UNICEF through to the British Council. We had two young technicians to help us, as our double-bridge marionette stage takes a good three hours to rig. We moved venues regularly with the festival, travelling to the Golan Heights in the north, then to Hebron, Nablus, Ramallah and Jericho, and finally to the most memorable place, Gaza.

Adam on the stage that had to be put up and down

The "Gaza Strip", as it was known during World War II, is a grim desert place and makes for a dreary journey. Getting there is a complex affair. We were booked to perform in a school in Gaza itself and set out with our two helpers. After passing through a number of roadblocks

Changing the number plate

manned by Israeli soldiers, we stopped in a car park where our helpers changed the number plates on our vehicle. We were told this was necessary in order to be allowed into Gaza.

This alarmed us somewhat, but Imad Mitwali, one of the technicians, of whom more later, told us that we would be stopped and possibly prevented from continuing our journey if we did not do this.

The Gaza audience was boisterous but delighted with both *The Birdman* and *Monkey Business*, and after the performance we were treated to an enormous meal of roast lamb surrounded by rice and almonds. The visit to Gaza was unforgettable, but not one that a person would choose to go through a second time – unless you were giving an experience to the children who live there.

Our destination

In between visits to schools and venues in other Palestinian towns, we were entertained by the El Hakawati team with lunches and dinners at the theatre, or sightseeing trips into the ancient city or to famous sites in the area. One of these excursions was a picnic at the Dead Sea. We set out in daylight, swam in the strange salty water and, as darkness fell, a huge fire was lit on the beach for barbecuing lamb and goat.

Floating in the Dead Sea

After the feast, the team brought out their instruments (ouds and drums) to play traditional tunes. As soon as the music started, the men leapt to their feet and danced with each other in a completely spontaneous way, singing and clapping. Can you imagine Englishmen doing that? In spite of the tension and restrictions in their lives, Palestinians know how to enjoy themselves. They have a great tradition of music, poetry and dance. Women are as prominent as men in their contributions to these fields, especially poetry.

That first visit, with Adam, was to be the first of many. We kept up our relationship with Jamal and returned to play in festivals in 1995, 1997 and 2000.

On the subsequent visits, first our daughter Natasha came with us and then Kate, both of whom performed in the rod shows that we took instead of a marionette

Juliet, Jamal and Gren

Kate and Kevin Griffiths

stage. The later visits varied in terms of the level of tension in the country and the severity of "stop and search" at roadblocks and questioning by armed police or soldiers as we travelled around the West Bank.

On these trips, we also gave shadow puppet workshops for teachers, so it was a great advantage to have our skilled daughters and other experienced puppeteers with us, including Rachel Leonard and Kevin Griffiths, both former trainees. Rachel went on to perform in the successful National Theatre production of *War Horse* and Kevin won a BAFTA award for the animated TV series *Old Bear Stories*.

Even a short trip in Palestine is arduous and occasionally we were prevented from reaching our destination. The Palestinians took it in their stride and if we asked them about it they would simply remark, "same shit, different day", or similar.

During one of the visits in the nineties, Imad Mitwali, who we had met on our first trip and had worked with us ever since, asked if he could come and work with us in the UK. His ambition was to start a touring puppet theatre and he was particularly interested in marionettes. We considered his request on our return and decided we could offer him an internship or extended workshop in marionette construction. Both parties approached the British Council, Imad in Jerusalem and us in London. Finally, our plans came good and Imad arrived to stay and work with us in spring 2000. Juliet remembers his visit:

Our West Bank audience

The crew on tour: Juliet, stagehand, Natasha, Imad Mitwali

"On arrival, Imad had to adjust to a London way of life, which basically meant not living in a war zone. The change was such that he found it very hard to do anything at all except talk, sleep and smoke, but in the final few days he made a marionette with Gren's help, the first for his theatre. After our first trip to Pakistan in 1982, a young artist, Karim Khan, had come to work with us for several months, so we knew about the difficulties experienced in moving from one country and culture to another. Pace seems to be a key thing; I always remember watching the London traffic, after being in Pakistan for a month, and thinking I had never seen anything so sedate and quiet. Karim went on to make his life here and continued with his ice carving.

Imad and his puppet in the London workshop

Imad went on to produce his first marionette drama from a Persian fable, and two years later we went back to Jerusalem to help him stage it. It was altogether a different trip for us. No puppets or staging to be transported, just ourselves and our knowledge to be shared. We spent an intense ten days mounting and staging the play with Imad and Hella, his wife and partner. On the last evening there was an opening performance for an invited audience, including representatives from the British Council. We were as nervous as Imad, wanting the ancient art form to touch down gently and proliferate in a new land. Imad went on to make a touring theatre in a truck that he took all over the West Bank, calling his theatre Movingstage. The show was later performed before Yasser Arafat, the Palestinian leader."

Many years later Imad arranged a visit for Hella and his son to visit Scotland to learn about shadow puppets with Colleen Magennis.

Dining with Imad and family

Chapter 19

Fun and Games

Oh, I get by with a little help from my friends,
Mm, I get high with a little help from my friends.
John Lennon and Paul McCartney
With a Little Help from my Friends (1967)

After Lahore and the Gaza Strip, we were happy to get back to London in time for Christmas and the chance to take new plans and ideas forward into 1993.

We managed to hire a space to rehearse *All He Fears* in the derelict German Hospital in Hackney. Mike Pearce, who had toured with us in Greece, was engaged to direct. Although he wasn't experienced with puppets he did have a couple of prize-winning films under his belt. It was very stimulating seeing all the ideas coming together like a giant jigsaw. The production began to take shape and finally we were ready to show it to Howard. He entered the old hospital very suspiciously, waiting to be attacked by leftover bugs and germs!

With all the elements in place, we sat him down and said that we would prefer to have notes at the end of the performance rather than at half-time. His riposte – "If I am still here" – was a big shock for us! He did stay, and he gave us some useful notes.

The first performance was scheduled to take place at the Brighton Pavilion Theatre, as part of the Brighton Festival. It was exciting but daunting and we set off with nervous anticipation. The company consisted of Gren, Juliet, our daughter Kate and puppeteer Nancy Clark who had trained with us. Among the audience were Howard, Ian McDiarmid and composer Matthew Scott; all went well, and we emerged triumphant and happy. The piece was well received, and we went on to tour the show at several venues in the south.

As well as this achievement, the most joyous event of summer 1993 was the arrival of our second grandson, Joshua. Before his birth, Kate, his mother, had valiantly stayed the course for our visit to Brighton for the premiere, followed by Plymouth's Drum Theatre in the West Country.

The new stage undressed, with Jolyon (left) and Juliet (right); note the policeman on the stage

Following the summer dates, we went north, taking in Sheffield, York, Liverpool and other venues during the very cold November of 1993. It was extremely hard work, as the new stage took at least five hours to rig and and dress, the weather was terrible. Blizzards and heavy snow made driving hard going as we were towing a large trailer. Inevitably we broke down and faced the extra stress of trying to reach venues in time and cover our costs; all part of the touring lifestyle. But, of course, there were also the high moments when audiences came backstage after a performance to tell us that the power of the puppet had carried the extraordinary content of Howard's play.

Outings for the sake of enjoyment were *verboten*, not by any written rule or pre-arranged planning, but simply due to our pure enthusiasm and desire to create a successful show. It is impossible to know why we had the motivation to do what we were doing. Certainly, it wasn't fame that we were after, or riches, but seemingly just an inner drive to create and present marionette theatre. It was as Shakespeare wrote in *Hamlet*: "Though this be madness, yet there is method in 't".

Before touring north in the autumn of 1993, we adapted *All He Fears* for the barge stage, so we could take it out on the annual river tour and present it as our evening production throughout the summer. It was a difficult task but we persevered and once the job was complete, we felt more confident and pleased with the way the show matured on the barge. Using the barge was more relaxing than touring to different venues, where you didn't know what difficulties you may have to deal with from day to day; we also wanted to present the show in London early in 1994 at our Little Venice mooring, so we were prepared in good time.

As we packed up after the last performance of the land tour we realised that Howard had not finished with us yet – the London season

Botius and Horse in the underworld

on the barge was yet to come – but fortunately the struggles of touring were over. We could now look forward to Christmas and a bit of merriment, despite the discipline required in order to get the barge up and running after our touring sojourn. We opened the half-term season on the barge towards the end of October 1993 with *Tales from Aesop* and followed it up with a Christmas show based on Brer Rabbit having a Father Christmas issue with Brer Fox. We are happy to report that every performance on this run was sold out. This was followed by a run of *The Flight of Babuscha Baboon*, which brought us the same success. Neither of us remembers riding high at the time, but as we write, 25 years on, the same show has just opened, and we hope for the same success. One of the beauties of the marionette is that you can put it to sleep and years later re-stage the show.

In early March 1994 we opened *All He Fears* on the barge at Little Venice for an evening run of three weeks. We did our best with press releases and were rewarded by a big piece of editorial in *Time Out*, written by James Christopher, before the show opened. Howard's work was popular at the time and critics from the big papers all came along. We received some wonderful reviews. It did the trick. We were full for the entire run and all of us really enjoyed it. It was so much nicer performing on the barge, more like being at home, and the show was better for it.

One evening during the London run, we had a visit from Michael Raab, dramaturg of a theatre in Mainz, Germany, who was in London choosing plays for a drama festival to take place in May. We were thrilled when he chose *All He Fears* to be part of it. From the start, the job was pure luxury. Firstly, we were funded (readily) by the British Council, which also arranged transport by road and air for all our staging and ourselves. All we had to do was arrive at the airport with a small bag! In Mainz, our host offered us wonderful hospitality and attention, and the German audiences just loved Howard's bleak, dark, humorous writing. Howard's plays are now, seemingly, more popular in Europe and, strangely, in Australia, than in the UK.

The trip to Mainz was a good way to end the two-year run of touring, although we did have to give one more performance on the touring stage at Reading Festival. Since then we have run successful evening seasons of *All He Fears* in Richmond upon Thames and for the Suspense Festival of puppetry

Babuscha and Elly

in London. It was an exciting time adapting the Barker production for presentation on the barge and we became aware that it attracted a new fringe theatre audience that was experiencing puppet theatre for the first time.

1994 was not only the year of the Barker play but a year to be feared, especially if one was the owner of a very old vessel without wings. It was a year of much activity that began in earnest with shows for the spring followed by the annual tour up the Thames. The last shows of the London season were on the bank holiday weekend during the Inland Waterways Festival, finishing on June 3. We set off immediately along the canal to join the river at Brentford, a strenuous journey in itself but with a sense of great relief as one turns into the wonderful, wide and deep River Thames.

The journey from Little Venice to our mooring near Caversham, abutting Reading, took us about two weeks. The season was well planned and went well. From there we moved downstream to Henley for the festival, which had been the highlight of the year for the past twelve years and we were not going to change our collective opinions on that point. No sooner did we reach Henley than we gathered our friends around and the merriment began.

Friends on a good evening
At the very back (unseen):
Andy Doyle and Sue Beattie;
second row: Louise Middleton,
Mark Ashley, Kate and
Natasha Middleton, Paul Bijl;
front row: Amanda Shaw, Jan Pitt

It is difficult to know why Andy Doyle cannot be seen in the picture because he was the life and soul of the party and is well over six feet tall! Sue Beattie, a trainee some years back, introduced Andy to us. He came to visit Sue on the barge and without hesitation started to polish the brass and blacken the coal stoves that were used at the time.

Since then Andy has contributed hours of his time to the barge, from ushering people in to performances at the festival to helping move the barge and putting the roof up and down. Not long after we met Andy he teamed up with Jan Pitt, who had been one of our early lodgers, and between them they have produced two children. All four are now part of the circle of close friends who give their talents, time and labour regularly to the barge.

Andy Doyle and first child Jasmine   *Jan Pitt with second child Ben*
The Pitt-Doyles grew up with the barge and company

Henley was followed by Marlow and a weekend at Cliveden; we then moved off the river and performed at a festival in Ealing on the canal before heading back on the river to Richmond. It was a full, rounded tour, performing most days and barging on the rest. Paul Bijl, raised on a boat at Little Venice, became a regular helper every summer when we were moving on the river. He was an excellent waterman and could tie a bowline in a split second in an emergency. By this time, we were moving two barges every year as we had *Eroda* with us for accommodation, as well as the puppet barge. Paul would steer one or other vessel and over the years he taught us many a useful tip about tides, currents and anchorage. We also had wonderful help from our other boating friends, Martin Cottis and Charlie Tymms, both artists who lived on the water and came and moved barges with us when we needed help. They subsequently set up some residential moorings on the Thames below Tower Bridge, where they live on their beautiful barge *Albatross*. We finished the summer tour on October 10, 1994 after 128 days of performing and moving the barge. Exactly 3115 tickets were sold during that summer.

We then had to face the canal journey back to Little Venice and set up for the winter season – as ever, not an easy prospect but we were young and had our young trainee, Anna Ingleby, with us making good progress. We arrived at a deep lock with double sluice gates. Unfortunately Anna opened the top sluices first, which flooded the front area of the puppet barge because the portholes were open. This in itself was not a disaster but the effect would prove significant later. We motored on, arriving at Little Venice two days later.

Having mopped up the water from the lock spillage we erected the roof in the late afternoon and said goodbye to Paul Bijl, Andy Doyle and our daughter Natasha, who had been helping with the roof. We went off for fish and chips feeling pleased to be back and that everything was in order. Or so we thought!

We returned to the barge well-fed and happy. The roof was up and all was ready for the next season, with the first performance scheduled for October 23, giving us a ten-day break to recover and prepare. We entered the barge only to discover with horror that the water had returned! After much contemplation, we realised that it was not the water from the sluice but new water coming in from beneath and that there must be a hole in the bottom of the boat – more shock. The implications were horrid and very difficult to accept.

We had to make a plan. First we had to get through the night. To do this we decided that we would take it in two-hourly shifts to pump out the water. After a disturbed night we were up early and conceived a modus operandi. The first thing was to phone around to try and find a dry dock that could accommodate the barge. Next, we needed to take the roof down. With morale low and worries about our situation, particularly the cost of it, we set off back up the canal. It is hard to imagine how we managed that, but manage it we did. Down came the roof and back along the canal we sailed, returning to Brentford where we met Ted Leppard from Eel Pie Island Slipways – and what a saviour he was. He looked at the barge, assessed the problem, said he could cope with it and followed up with instructions.

We were relieved to get to the yard, where we were met by a tall, skinny man from Calcutta holding out a long pole with a hook. He shouted to us in a broad Indian accent, "Attach a rope!" We jumped to and followed instructions, whereupon he ran the rope around a bollard and secured the barge.

Not long after that the tide went out and the barge was winched up, on wooden logs, into the dry dock. The day had ended and we were safely in Ted's hands and he sent us off to have dinner in Twickenham, giving us instructions on how to get back into the yard. When we returned some hours later, we found our way in, but now the place was totally quiet, dark and deserted. What a change from earlier on, when it had been humming with noise and activity. Now it was eerie and silent as we climbed the long ladder up onto the barge and lit our oil lamps to find our way to bed. We slept well, despite the barge being tipped up at quite

Juliet on the front deck in the dry dock

a steep angle. We woke early next morning to the deafening sound of hammers hitting metal, grinders and welders going full tilt, all mixed with shouts and whistling.

The next two days were spent hanging around while Ted found the leak, a loose rivet in the bottom. He welded a plate on top of the damaged spot and pronounced that all was well and we could be off on the next tide.

It was just getting dark when the tide began to move. As Gren started the engine, diesel fuel spurted out of the copper pipe where it entered the diesel pump. Does the horror never stop? We have no explanation for why this happened but discovered that there was a damaged olive in the connection to the pump. Ted had no spares so Gren made a plan to get a spare from *Eroda,* our second boat, moored at Richmond.

Ted gave us a lift to Richmond where we managed to row across the river on, by now, a fast-flowing tide, and get ourselves onto the boat. Gren removed the relevant part from the engine. We rowed back across the incoming tide, found a taxi and got back to Eel Pie, installed the replacement part and started the engine. All was well and we left Eel Pie just as the tide was turning. We made for Richmond, where we planned to moor up for the night.

By the time we got to Richmond the tide had turned and was running fast. Gren turned the barge mid-river and came back up against the current, but Juliet would have to jump off the barge onto the pontoon with a rope and get a turn on the bollard. How we managed to moor up in the dark, safely, with a fast-running tide, is a mystery. Sometimes necessity provides extra adrenalin and saves you, as it did for us. This little operation was a nightmare. The tides on the Thames can be very dangerous – even Royal Navy vessels have been in trouble, so much so that in one case the Captain lost his job.

The next day we set off back to Little Venice – just the two of us – and got back safely with our jobs intact!

The puppet Barge moored at Little Venice

The Puppet Barge flaunts its swanky new cover

Interior of Puppet Barge – the show is about to begin

Gren and Juliet in their workshop

"All of the things I cannot put into words."
Graffiti

The barge on the Regent's Canal in Hackney, heading back to Little Venice

Passing the "hanging woods" on the Cliveden Reach of the River Thames

Puppet Barge entering Limehouse after the summer tour
On the tiller: Paul Bijl & Amy Hazeldine
Front deck: Bea Pentney, Juliet, Rob, Stan, Simon Oatley

Family caught together for one fiftieth of a second
Back row: Joshua, Rob, Tom
Front row: Gren, Juliet, Stan, Natasha, Louise, Kate

Chapter 20

Action and Play

> *It is vain to say human beings ought to be*
> *satisfied with tranquillity: they must have action;*
> *and they will make it if they cannot find it.*
> **Charlotte Brontë**
> *Jane Eyre (1847)*

News Bunny, the station mascot of the TV station L!VE TV, was a timely saviour of the Puppet Barge and Movingstage Marionette Company. One day late in 1995, a call came from the office of Mr Kelvin MacKenzie, L!VE TV boss, regarding a puppet project that he, former editor of *The Sun* newspaper and publicity-seeking expert, wanted to discuss. Juliet took the call and made the appointment. It wasn't long before she was on her way to Canary Wharf where L!VE TV had their studio and offices. Kelvin was a tough journalist turned TV boss, best known for his time at *The Sun*, between 1981 and 1994, when the paper had the largest circulation in the United Kingdom. Juliet continues the story:

"I had been asked on the phone whether we would be interested in making a puppet that could appear with the news broadcasts. At this stage I had no idea what sort of puppet they wanted or what it would be required to do, so it was with some trepidation that I made my way to Canary Wharf, wondering what we had got ourselves into.

L!VE TV had its studios on the 29th floor, so after a long lift ride, I arrived and was shown into Nick Ferrari's office. Nick, who was second-in-command at the time, was very pleasant and explained that they would like a large soft puppet that could be operated by one puppeteer and that would be able to make gestures showing how it felt about the news items

– pleased or displeased. He asked me to send them some designs, and they would make a decision as soon as they had them.

I sent the drawings off in the next day or two and got a call back immediately saying they liked them and would we go ahead and make the puppet. I had managed to produce a cartoonish character that avoided being anything like Peter Rabbit, Brer Rabbit or Bugs Bunny, the obvious classics, but was cheeky and cute without being a fluffy toy. When made, it could flick its ears up and down, make the thumbs up or down sign and wink its eyes.

I set off to Canary Wharf again, rabbit in bag, to 'demo' it. Nick and Kelvin were both there this time, and I remember very clearly the response I got as they turned on a piece of newsreel and I ad-libbed the gestures with the puppet. They both fell about laughing and clapped each other on the back like a couple of schoolboys, and then ran out into the studio calling other people to come and watch. I was rather flattered – it is always nice to have an appreciative audience – but realised at the same time that they were chuffed with themselves at having come up with a good idea.

The next visit was to make a pilot film with a real newsreader. The date was arranged but unfortunately I had fallen off my bike and broken my shoulder, so I had to teach another puppeteer how to operate the bunny. We went to L!VE TV together and I remember Kelvin saying, 'What's wrong with you, then?' When I told him, he replied, 'What on earth are you doing on a bike at your age?' Outrageous!

At this point Kelvin and Nick suddenly decided that they didn't want a puppet after all, and that instead the entire design should be transferred into a body costume. I think this was because they realised that a puppeteer would have to be engaged on a daily basis, whereas to put one of their runners into the suit would cost much less. Also, while a puppet's gestures require the skills of a puppeteer, it would not be so difficult for a human to make News Bunny gestures while wearing a costume.

By now we had received initial payments for the puppet design and making, but on one of my visits Nick had casually mentioned that a legal agreement was being prepared by their lawyers, allowing L!VE TV the rights to use News Bunny in any way, which we would need to agree to. After a phone call from L!VE TV's lawyers, Gren and I agreed that we needed some heavy-duty legal advice to guide us over the next steps and asked our good friend and accountant Jeffrey Lent to help us. Thank goodness we did. Jeff became our accountant when he was just about to qualify. Since that time, he had become very successful and helped us in many ways. At this point he recommended an entertainments lawyer who would sort us out. We never did meet the lawyer; he negotiated a buy-out fee with the L!VE TV management by phone, over the course of just three calls. The deal he made paid for his fee and earned us £26,000!

During this period Gren was studying a book entitled *Teach Yourself Business* and had learned about working capital. At that point our working capital was an overdraft of some £10,000. This was very expensive, but after News Bunny's miraculous transformation from a puppet into a half-human, half-rabbit character of immense personality, we could bring our bank problems to a close.

We paid off the overdraft and left £10,000 in the current account – this was designated our working capital, none of which was to be used other than for the monthly expenses incurred by the company. The money was to be replaced during the month by the income from the box office receipts. The business was saved and has continued to grow."

In the meantime, the giant rabbit would appear during news bulletins and mime actions related to what the newsreader was saying. Good news would be greeted with an enthusiastic thumbs-up, while during bad news the bunny would hang his head, drop his ears and look sad. Up until this point almost all UK TV news was presented in a serious manner; the bunny helped pave the way for subsequent more relaxed approaches to news presentation.

Wikipedia reports that the impact of News Bunny has been the subject of academic research.

Despite the channel's poor ratings News Bunny became a national cult figure,

News Bunny 1996–1999

attracting much tabloid and other media interest, and being mentioned in Parliament. Aside from his studio appearances News Bunny regularly appeared alongside politicians, pop stars and royalty, many of whom would have preferred to avoid him. These appearances usually occurred during outside broadcasts and publicity stunts. The Bunny gate-crashed an official visit by Michael Heseltine to Canary Wharf in 1996, and famously secured 8 seconds with Tony Blair.

News Bunny also stood for Parliament representing the "L!VE TV Party" in the South East Staffordshire by-election, 1996, polling 85 votes. In order to do this, a Mirror Group employee had to change his name to "News Bunny" for the purposes of the election. According to an apocryphal story circulating among journalists at the time, during the campaign a stunt went wrong and the hapless hack was arrested for obstruction. As there was a police case pending against him, he was unable to change his name back for some time and had to live as "Mr N. Bunny" for weeks longer than he had expected.

News Bunny went off air with L!VE TV in 1999 and is now owned by Vauxhall-based ETV, founded by L!VE's former management team. The character made a brief revival during their 2003 relaunch of the station on Sky Digital.

It is thanks to Wikipedia that the bunny's short life is recorded for posterity. Had News Bunny been living in the wild, his lifespan would have been a miserable three years.

Chapter 21

Puppet Power

Whatever happens we have got
The Maxim gun, and they have not.
Hilaire Belloc *(1870–1953)*
The Modern Traveller (1898)

We had been trying to buy a Burmese tiger to add to our collection of Burmese puppets. We did eventually acquire one through an antique dealer who made regular trips to Myanmar. It now sits in the barge guarding the way to the loo. During the hunt for our tiger we learned about a marionettist who lived in Myanmar's capital, Yangon. This inspirational true story was written by American journalist, Will Doig, who has kindly given us permission to re-tell it here:

"The map appeared in my inbox attached to an email with instructions to arrive at 5 p.m. It was signed, "With best wishes and regards, U Htwe & Aunty OO."

When I showed the map to my taxi driver he squinted at it sceptically, then let me out on a dirt street far from Yangon's neon hotels. Stray dogs sheltered in the late-day shadows, and a teenager wrenched on a beat-up Yamaha motorbike. By the side of the road, a young monk tended a smoldering garbage fire.

"You look for puppets?" the monk asked. He pointed to a ramshackle three-story building and told me to pull the blue string. It rang a bell on the balcony, and moments later, Khin Maung Htwe appeared at the door.

The nightly puppet show performed at Htwe's residence (his name is pronounced "Tway") is one of the hidden marvels of Myanmar's raucous capital city.

Here in the nation's cultural nerve center, the trauma of 52 years of oppression is giving way to a palpable sense of cautious exhilaration. With human rights icon Aung San Suu Kyi emceeing the fledgling democracy's return to the world stage, an energetic arts scene is finally awakening from a long, totalitarian-induced sleep.

Htwe is an unlikely player in this process. On September 18, 2001, he was sailing into New York Harbor when the Coast Guard intercepted his vessel. Beneath a sky still tinged with the smoke of the 9/11 attacks, for two hours a team of skittish armed agents searched the Siemens container ship on which he worked as an ocean navigator. Back home in Myanmar, his country was changing just as fast as America, as five decades of senseless brutal military rule sputtered to a messy close.

A year after his Coast Guard encounter, Htwe quit the seafaring job he'd held for 18 years and returned home to help raise his 5-year-old daughter amid the tumult. When he returned, he would also find a new sense of purpose in reviving a centuries-old form of theater that was once a keystone of the Burmese art scene.

He got the idea when he bought a microbus and turned it into a tour van. "While driving tourists, I visited other cities—Mandalay, Bagan— and saw puppetry in these places. But I never saw it in Yangon." Htwe thought this would have saddened his mother, who had instilled in him a love of the theater, taking him to all-night performances at the country's pagoda festivals. "Then I read a book about puppetry and learned it was one of Myanmar's original performing arts," he says, "a tradition that dates back hundreds of years."

In the 15th century, traditional Burmese puppet theater was performed for the royal families of what was then Southeast Asia's mighty Taungoo Empire. Years later, when British colonists linked up the country with railroads, puppeteer troupes took their shows on the road, delighting audiences in villages throughout the countryside. The 500-year-old tradition was curtailed in 1962 when the military seized power in a *coup d'état* and walled off Myanmar from the outside world.

According to Htwe, the generals were so upset about being called a puppet government that they went so far as to ban the word "puppet" from being printed in newspapers.

After crackdowns on protests rocked the country in 1988, the government shut down Yangon's biggest pagoda festival, as well as the puppet shows that had long been a part of it. By the time Htwe

Will Doig among the puppets

returned to Yangon, puppetry had all but vanished from the capital. He set to work bringing it back, renting a theater, hiring puppeteers, and choreographing shows. But the $500-per-month rent and puppeteers' salaries proved unsustainable.

"I lost a lot of money," he says. "I sold my car to keep things going." In 2008, he stumbled upon a free performance space, but it was destroyed later that year—along with all of his puppets—when Cyclone Nargis struck Myanmar, claiming 140,000 lives.

"My friends said, 'You'll be back on a boat in three years,'" he says. "It was hard. We couldn't afford to send my daughter to a good school. My mother-in-law told me to go back to sea." Instead, Htwe's wife sold her jewelry so they could construct a new set of puppets. And then, a stroke of good fortune arrived from an unexpected place: the United Arab Emirates.

Flush with money but not much art, the UAE invited Htwe to Dubai, where he put on his puppet show at a festival, in a children's area called the Amusement Zone. In Dubai, he met a hotel manager and struck a deal for a six-month profit-sharing residency. When it ended, he returned to Yangon and negotiated a similar arrangement with a lakeside restaurant.

It was just the boost he needed, but still not enough to keep him solvent. And so, he and his family leveraged the one space that was entirely under their control: their apartment in Yangon. Today, every inch of Htwe's living room has been converted into a theater. Violet curtains frame a stage opposite rows of chairs elevated onto risers. Spotlights and amplifiers, controlled from behind the curtain, flank the stage. The space accommodates 10 audience members, some of whom are already seated when I arrive, including two young Filipino men who are here because of Miss Myanmar, who, at this year's Miss Universe pageant, dressed as a traditional Burmese puppet. The contestant, a stunning 24-year-old named Htet Htet Htun, walked away with the Best Costume prize, not to mention adoring press coverage for her commitment to her country's heritage.

Htwe – photo by Will Doig

Soon the lights dim and the puppets take the stage: Marionettes dangled in front of a black curtain that partially hides the puppeteer pulling the strings. Traditional Burmese puppet shows run from sunset to sunrise; mercifully, Htwe's show is a 45-minute version of these nocturnal ones. It's composed of a series of vignettes drawn from Jataka tales, stories of the Buddha's previous incarnations. In one vignette, two ogres—one representing evil, the other virtue—battle in the jungle. In another, a mystical healer plays a flute that cures diseases. Htwe, his wife, and his son and daughter expertly manipulate the marionettes, each of which has 18 strings that move everything from the puppets' feet to their eyebrows. It's a truly dexterous performance, and hard not to watch the puppeteers' fingers as the puppets fight, dance, and fall in love.

At the end of the show, we're invited backstage. Behind the curtain is a cramped, rundown apartment consisting of two bedrooms and a tiny kitchen. It's a jarring reminder that this family has given up nearly everything—including half their home—to put on puppet shows for crowds of less than 10, in a neighborhood that taxis can't find. The notion suddenly seems insane, but Htwe doesn't see it that way. He's now been doing this for so long that it's simply become his life, unorthodox as it may appear. "I cannot go back to sea," he says. "I'm the director. My wife is the manager. In five years, my daughter will take my place. Five years after that, my son will take her place." And if the show becomes financially unsustainable? He looks at the family photos hanging on the walls: his kids playing by a marsh, a portrait of him in his sailor's uniform. "If we are not successful in five years, then we'll stop," he says. "Our visibility is growing. These days, we get an audience nearly every day as word continues to spread online."

He's waiting for his show to catch fire, to reignite a passion for traditional puppetry in modern Yangon, a city racing toward the future for the first time in half a century."

Burmese puppets on the barge

Our own Burmese puppets sit quietly on the barge while it journeys slowly up the Thames. We know they are genuine Burmese because they have their genitals carved into the lower part of the body. As far as we know, it is to carry the spirit of the puppet forwards.

Chapter 22

Movement

We know what happens to people who stay
in the middle of the road. They get run down.
Aneurin Bevan
The Observer (December 6, 1953)

It seems that there is always a moment – whether at a social occasion, when undertaking an artistic adventure, on holiday or running a business enterprise – when the fun stops and you are forced to come to grips with a new situation, which may sometimes be threatening. After two or three years of mooring outside Bamber Gascoigne's boathouse, we were forced to move on. The access for the public wasn't good enough; we needed a floating gangway that would adjust with the tide.

Not far upstream from Bamber's house was the White Cross, a popular pub and meeting place for Richmond groovers and Twickenham rugby players, managed, at the time, by Denise and Piers, a pleasant young couple who owned a large Portuguese water dog. It was to them we turned for a mooring, as there was a handsome pontoon opposite the pub. They told us that the pontoon was owned by Turk Launches, a well-known Thames passenger boat company owned and run by Mr Turk, known locally as "Turkey". They also told us that Portuguese water dogs were used by the barges that carried rum and that when they were going to moor up, the dog would swim to the shore with the rope in its mouth, give a turn around the bollard and swim back delivering the end to the bargee!

Denise and Piers gave us permission to draw power from the pub and told us the times when Turk's used the pontoon. Armed with this knowledge, we made contact with Mr Turk who gave us permission to moor there from September 1 onwards, as the passenger boat service stopped at the end of August. This mooring lasted for a few years before Turkey decided that he wanted to extend his season. Boat wedding receptions were becoming fashionable and we were in the way, so we had to move on.

At around this time Juliet attended a lecture given by Captain Bull, head of the Port of London Authority, on the history of the "Richmond curtain". Following the talk, she spoke to him briefly. This meeting encouraged us to ask him for his help and advice regarding our mooring problem and Gren subsequently got in touch. Captain Bull suggested we contacted Peter Ellis, who had taken over some moorings from his father in Petersham, a riverside stretch just upstream from the White Cross.

Upon visiting him and the moorings we found Peter to be a genuine character in many ways. He had the use of an old boathouse overlooking the moorings, which was a real Aladdin's cave packed full of old engines, boat parts, chandlery of every description and even a vintage Humber Super Snipe car. He had also, until recently, run a second-hand bookstall outside the boathouse every Saturday. When we turned up, we explained about the theatre and he showed us the old pontoon where we could moor for a season, which he said would be no problem. We shook hands and left, but soon realised that no mention had been made about charges! We hesitated, but decided we must sort the matter out and returned. Peter mumbled something about what we could afford, and we quickly settled on a reasonable amount. He was always very fair. Thus the mooring was secured and barge life enhanced.

Slowly, we got to know him, together with his girlfriend Judy. Sadly, Peter was struck with terminal cancer some years later. Before he passed on he sold us the licence for the moorings, which was a life-changing deal. We struck a good bargain. Although we had to pay him thousands in cash with no paperwork, he was true to his word and the PLA issued us with a new licence.

As well as a secure mooring for the Puppet Barge, this also gave us a "trot" of moorings on piles and buoys on both sides of the river, which we were able to sublet to boat owners. This is a wonderfully beneficial sideline that supports the Puppet Barge by making a small profit each year. Having the income from the moorings has enabled us to make new shows and employ puppeteers over the years without depending on arts funding. The Richmond audience are top-class theatregoers and supporters of the arts generally. The river is also a lot of fun for swimming and boating when we are off duty.

John Reed and Peter, "The Quiet Man"

We have learned a fair amount about the river, the people that work on it and the protocol when dealing with the Authority, and so we have been able to manage the moorings with some success. Juliet is in charge and works closely with John Reed, our resident waterman, who is well known on the river and is in touch with what is happening on a day-to-day basis. John uses the moorings for his own wheeling and dealing and we both get on with him, offering him free use of the moorings in return for his services. Barry Leader, a former gravedigger turned parks warden, now retired, also has a boat on the patch. He is a great asset in looking after the place, so he also has a free mooring. So too does Pete, "The Quiet Man", who is very handy but does not say a lot.

The Richmond stretch of water is tidal, but the "curtain" is there to stop the water draining off completely at low tide. The curtain, which acts as a dam wall, is raised two hours before high tide and then closed again two hours after the tide has turned, thus keeping a good level of water in the river. Once a year in November the "curtain" is left open and the water is allowed to flow out naturally. At low tide the river presents itself as a stream and one can almost walk across it.

After years of touring the upper Thames all summer we have, since 2009, cut down the distance we travel and now spend mid-July to early October in Richmond every year – our summer home. The place is a fashionable town littered with boutiques, pubs and restaurants, inhabited by trendy people such as Mick Jagger, writers, actors and all manner

The November "run off"

of celebrities. It is an excellent place for a sophisticated audience; the performances are often sold out and the shows are always appreciated.

Peter Ellis went on to buy a modern boat which he moored in Shepperton Marina and spent his last years there. We held his wake on our barge *Eroda*, and, like all wakes, it was a merry affair tinged with sadness. Peter had helped us in so many ways, including finding an old steam dredger that now serves as a store and pontoon. The engines and dredging machinery had been removed and a lot of Thames mud replaced the works. We soon put the mud back into the river and got the boat up to scratch, including a smart wooden deck installed by The Quiet Man.

Peter and dog Nipper

The lamp post

Finding a reliable power supply for the barge was and still is a terrible problem, be it in Henley, Richmond or Little Venice, where we have a 16-amp outlet supplied by the Canal Trust. Even this source can give trouble.

In Richmond, Nigel Cutting, the arts officer at the time, introduced us to Bob Pike, the boss of the council works department. Bob, an unusually helpful man, installed a power supply for us on a lamp post! Nigel, who managed to sport a tan all year round, rewarded us with an annual grant that was withdrawn when he left the council and the arts department moved to a stately home, Orleans House – not a good move for us, or the Richmond citizens.

Downstream from Richmond, at Isleworth, there is a particularly useful mooring where one can tie up and check the propeller and paint the section of the hull that is usually below the water line.

When the tide goes out the barge is high and dry for about four hours, when the tasks can be done. To paint the hull takes about three tides. When the tide comes in, time is spent in the pub, cooking dinner or just lying about resting before the long hard canal journey that lies ahead. Sometimes the barge has to go into dry dock at Brentford

Isleworth – Juliet can be seen painting

for repairs to the hull. This is rather an expensive operation that has to be avoided except in extreme circumstances. It is not every year that the barge has to have the Isleworth treatment.

When one starts on the journey home, whether it is from Isleworth or Richmond, the departure needs careful timing, as getting into the canal at Brentford is very tricky if the tide is running at full strength. Once through the Thames Lock the stillness of the canal is a treat and it is easy to forget that the depth in various places is insufficient and that a two-day struggle lies ahead. This entails pushing and shoving, clearing the propeller and winding many locks as the barge climbs from sea level to Little Venice, at an altitude of 46 feet.

When we first started using the canal, it was very empty – not that there was no water in it, but rather there were barely any boats using it. Sometimes we would cruise along all day and feel as though we were on our own private waterway.

The condition of the canal has improved, sections are dredged occasionally but not as much as we would like. The sides of the canal and the towpaths are now looked after regularly, and planting has taken place together with management of the trees. Instead of factories, broken-down buildings, decay, rubble, muck and rubbish backing onto the canal, people are using the buildings and designing new structures, facing onto the water, which hugely improves the general outlook.

It is always wonderful to arrive safely back in Little Venice. It is a haven of peace after the general bleakness of the canal and the gruelling work of the long journey back.

Chapter 23

Party Party

In this best of possible worlds all is for the best.
Voltaire 1694 – 1778
Candide (1759)

Summer 1996 appeared out of nowhere and once again we found ourselves on the river heading towards Abingdon with a new show on board. We had left London soon after the first May bank holiday weekend and stopped at Walton-on-Thames for a short season, before tackling the journey up to Abingdon. The local arts officer in Abingdon had booked us primarily for the adult show *The River Girl* by Wendy Cope, with the added attraction of a talk and reading at one of the performances, to which Wendy kindly agreed. We also arranged to put on an exhibition of some puppets on the steel touring stage in Abingdon Museum.

After arriving we put the roof up and the two of us left Mhari Smith, the trainee, in charge and made our way back to London to fetch the stage and puppets for the exhibition. The night we were away, some lads undid the mooring lines, leaving the barge to sail towards the weir with Mhari asleep in the back cabin. Fortunately, the barge went aground, being anchored by the gangplank that was still attached. The incident caused some damage to said gangplank but Mhari was unhurt and had only woken up as the barge came to a stop with a jolt. We offered a £100 reward for any information leading to the arrest of the culprits, but they were never caught, and we had to get on with the job of knocking the aluminium gangplank back into shape.

Although Abingdon presented an attractive image of an English market town, underneath there were gangs of delinquent boys waiting for some sport, so that could be annoying, but we soon toughened up. Gren frightened them off by photographing them whenever they came near the barge.

We opened the season with a new show entitled *Red Riding Hood and the Wolf that tried to eat her*. Written by Deborah Jones, it had a wonderful twist and was beautifully voiced by actors Stephanie Fayerman, Philip Voss and our daughter Louise. Abingdon was soon over and the success of the shows, Wendy's visit plus our exhibition carried us forward for the whole summer.

Once again by some unknown source of magic (serious planning, negotiations and arrangements) we arrived in Henley for the festival not knowing that it was to be our last one. We had prepared a special show for a sophisticated audience entitled *The Decay of Lying*, based on a witty, wise and humorous essay written by Oscar Wilde. Perhaps it is a dissertation on how "true art" is required to lie (as in tell fibs), a skill that Oscar asserts is becoming sadly neglected as the fashion for lying has fallen into decay.

The script called for two puppets (named after his two sons, Vivian and Cyril) in conversation, and was supported by a series of high-resolution transparencies projected onto a background screen. The pictures either condemned or supported Oscar's theories as the argument progressed. Sadly, we underestimated the sophistication of the audience and the show did not go down well with everybody.

One person, on the way out, was heard to say to his friend, *"Sorry I put you through that"*.

We took it on the chin and carried on having fun and enjoying the different acts and happenings around the grounds; this included attending rehearsals during the day, meeting the various artists and generally being part of the "inside set".

Towards the end of the festival, the Artistic Director, Stewart Collins, very cleverly gave us our notice. Luckily, we were getting tired of making a different show, for the festival, every year so we were able to accept the notice without too much pain and get on and enjoy ourselves.

There was still much fun to be had and the rubbish skips were always worth investigating; we often rescued and recycled yards of cotton

All the people looking at the camera belong to the barge starting with Juliet and Jan Pitt on the left then Mark Ashley, Kate, Natasha and Andy. In the front row Nancy Perrin, Leslie Muggeridge and Louise

sheeting, cups and saucers and other restaurant items thrown away at the end of the festival week by the different catering companies.

Over the years, the local environmental officer, Mr Alibone, together with the Royal Berkshire Fire Brigade, knocked us into shape by insisting on all sorts of alterations that we should make, some of which were really petty, and others which made sense. The threat of an IRA attack was always in the air, particularly as Michael Heseltine was the Henley MP from 1974 through to 2001. During the Thatcher years he was a key minister in the cabinet, earning the nickname of Tarzan. When he retired, his wife declared, at some point, that, "It was quite fun being married to Johnny Weismuller". His *Spitting Image* puppet portrayed him as a camouflage-clad warrior reminiscent of the 1960s white British mercenary of the Congo, Colonel "Mad Mike".

One of the highlights of the festivals was to be had at the end of each one, when everyone had gone, apart from a few technicians who would be clearing up the lighting and other equipment. We would set out a large table in the grounds, or in a tent if bad weather was imminent, and proceed to have a wonderful lunch with all our friends and puppeteers. Somehow, we kept the festival dates going for fourteen years, not quite up to *Mousetrap* statistics but moving in the right direction.

Cover of the programme for our last year at Henley Festival

The loss of the Henley Festival booking did not stop us performing for the town for many years after we had been given the boot. We had fallen in love with the place and by coincidence had a lovely, close friend, Diana Trainor, whose father, George Haynes, lived in a big house fronting onto the river opposite the regatta winning post. Diana often visited George, who was an interesting, eccentric and generous man, and as a result many memorable times were enjoyed in his house. On several occasions we crossed the fast-flowing Thames in our little unstable dinghy, late at night and less than sober. We were, of course, never far from hard work; but everything is possible when one is below the age of eighty!

Following our 1996 adventures on the river, which started on May 25 and finished on October 13 in Richmond, we headed back to London with a slightly damaged ego owing to the loss of Henley Festival, but things never stand still.

At about this time, Penny Francis, the doyen of English puppetry, offered us the most wonderful gift, the management of Art of the Puppet Limited, a registered charity.

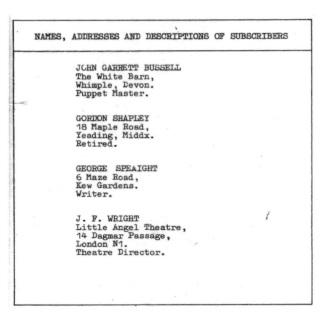

Copied from the Articles of Association of the Art of the Puppet Limited

The first subscribers to the charity were all well known and respected in the puppet business at the time. Jan Bussell passed our first show for the Festival in 1979. John Wright taught us how to run a theatre and George Speaight taught us the importance of history. Gordon Shapley introduced us to the Puppet Theatre Guild.

Taking over the charity has helped us enormously. All our school and education work is done through it and we are able to raise funds for the barge for the making of new productions and commissioning writers. Penny and Gren have had their differences over the years, especially when Penny published incorrect information about Barker's *All He Fears* and our relationship with the script. After confronting her with the error, she pleaded guilty and was forgiven. Her achievements in support of puppetry, including presenting two international puppet festivals in London, are fantastic and we only wish someone could follow in her footsteps and do the same again.

Penny's husband, the actor Derek Francis, had been a talented amateur puppet master and when he passed on Penny gave us some of his puppet gear, including a proscenium arch modelled by him, now on display in the foyer of the barge.

144

Having the income from the moorings provides a wonderful subsidy and has enabled us to make new shows and employ puppeteers over the years, without having to depend on arts funding. It has also given us a secure mooring for the barge for the summer season. The Richmond audiences are top class theatregoers and supporters of the arts generally. The river is also a lot of fun for swimming and boating when we are off duty.

By now the operation of the theatre was beginning to acquire a routine pattern, comprising a London season from October through to June/July, after which we would head up the Thames. Somehow it was easier without the discipline of the Henley Festival. The change from central London to rural Oxfordshire is always stimulating and it breaks the routine of the year. During this time, we take on two would-be puppeteers as trainees, which keeps the stable of marionette manipulators full.

Having arrived back in London, we opened the autumn season with *Red Riding Hood,* not seen in London before. It is an original and beautiful way of telling the traditional story. Not long after writing this play Deborah Jones emigrated to Scotland. She is now a recognised writer of drama there but is a loss to England.

As autumn turned into winter, in spite of having an efficient central heating system run on diesel oil, we really had to pull our weight to stay warm and attract an audience to the ice-bound barge in the snowy wastes of Little Venice. Luckily, we now had the excellent part-time help of Daphne O'Connell, administrator and publicity officer. Daphne had previously worked at the Royal Opera House, but now having a baby boy, she needed some less demanding hours of work. She was super-experienced and skilled in using every possible outlet to publicise our shows and it was she who encouraged us to ask Michael Palin, of Monty Python fame, to become our patron. We had met Michael through a friend, his sister-in-law Mary Burd, while we were on holiday in France one year, and on a few other social occasions. And so, we wrote to him and he accepted on the understanding that he would not be asked to do absolutely anything! We were more than happy to agree and from then on our status has increased. As Michael has become more and more famous, through his films, travel programmes, acting and writing, so we have grown and are very proud to have him as our patron.

The barge in winter at Little Venice

"To buy a barge and turn it into a theatre was imaginative and a little crazy, perfect qualifications for the interest of someone who'd written and performed Monty Python ... Maybe they will realise one last ambition and go international. Across the sea. Until then they will continue to use the highest standards of marionette theatre to entertain their audiences. Which is where I came in. And I'm glad I did."

Michael Palin

Chapter 24

A Close Shave at Cookham

If you can't ride bareback, don't join the circus.
From a speech in the House of Commons

The journeys up the Thames and back again veered between beautiful countryside and urban ugliness on the outskirts of London. We experienced peace and stress in equal measure and many emotions in between. The Cliveden Reach with its hilly green landscape on the right, known as the "hanging woods", and the stately house at the top of the hill overlooking the river, present a picture of beauty and tranquillity.

The Cliveden Reach going towards Cookham

The barge would weave between the islands in the middle of the river while we looked for a suitable place to moor up overnight. We did eventually find a favourite spot where we would enjoy an evening of fun, barbecues and swimming in the river. This made for a lovely stopover on the way upriver towards our first scheduled mooring.

The next lock after the Cliveden Reach is Cookham. The village of Cookham is famous for being the home and birthplace of artist Stanley Spencer, born in 1891; he was knighted in 1959 just before he died. His paintings often reflect aspects of Christianity, including his *Christ Preaching at Cookham Regatta* series.

One fine morning we were approaching the lock as the gates were opening and the lock-keeper waved us in. As we entered, Gren put the gear lever, known as a Morse control, into reverse to stop the boat, but all that happened was that the barge continued to go forward at an increased speed. Juliet tried to get a rope onto the bollard without success; we simply could not stop the boat. It went towards the top gates and she shouted to the trainee and our Stan, now rising four, who were both standing on the front deck, to sit down! A moment later the front of the barge hit the top gate with an almighty crash. The huge lock gates opened for a split second, showing a wall of water about a foot wide, some of which gushed onto the front deck, and then slammed shut. Stan and our trainee must have got one big fright. The lock-keeper jumped onto the boat and took Stan ashore immediately and the boat settled very quickly, leaving us all in a state of shock but unhurt.

After a long wait in the lock the engineers appeared and examined the gates. Fortunately, Cookham Lock, by some quirk of fate, has a double lock and we were in the lower one at the time of the crash. The engineers managed to fill our lock and open the damaged gates; we then pulled forward out of the lock and moored up above, where we began to recover. Gren examined the engine and drive and established that a pin had broken in the gearing unit, meaning it could not move from forward into reverse. It was a simple repair. He tried to point out the reason for the problem to the lock-keeper, who did not want to get involved in any way. After some time, we were ready to move on. Juliet had cycled to Bourne End where we were to pick up our daughter Louise and her boyfriend at the time, actor Dave Schaal.

When Gren arrived at Bourne End with the barge, we met up with Dave and Louise who were both dressed like Hollywood celebs, Dave with his Ray-Bans and Louise in a smart white dress. As we were mooring up, for some unknown reason, Dave stepped off the pontoon and fell straight into the river, losing his fancy sunglasses. Well, we were able to laugh about it afterwards, although it wasn't funny at the time.

As a consequence of the Cookham accident, the Thames Authority tried to sue us. A Lloyd's insurance assessor was called in and after a couple of inspections and an interrogation, he declared that, because the broken pin was not a serviceable part, it was not our fault, which was a huge relief. The Authority had tried to pin a huge bill on us for the repair of the lock gate, which included payment for the use of a "tea barge" for the workers. News of the accident made the big glossy boating magazines!

Once we had got the barges on the go again, we soon recovered and made our way upriver. Fortunately, no further horrible incidents occurred that year. Our first stop was Henley town, then Marlow and back down to Cliveden which, of course, reminded us of the whole Cookham adventure! Once through the lock we had to face mooring up at Cliveden for a weekend of performances with the National Trust. It was never easy getting into the mooring; the river flow was fast and the depth of the water wasn't too good. Then, of course, the labour of putting the roof up for only one weekend before having to take it down again was reason for a good moan.

Despite all this, the company really enjoyed the Cliveden dates; the wonderful grounds could be explored during the day as well as at night when the public had left and the animals came out to play.

Logistics were difficult, however – including getting power to the barge and having to borrow a long gangplank owing to the shallow water and consequent difficulty in getting close enough to the bank. We did get some real help from a chap we nicknamed Billy Bunter, but the National Trust was tricky to deal with. After the first years, during which we were invited by one of their events officers, things became awkward. In the beginning, we were "official" and had an individual to deal with. As well as performing for the general public, we were asked to give a special show for the Cliveden Club. This is a very exclusive group whose membership buys the very best treatment and attention, so we were rather flattered to

Cliveden woods – a fun place to explore

be included in their calendar of events. The members were brought down from Cliveden House by minibus and after the show, a sumptuous tea was set out next to the boathouse, including cakes, champagne and pink napkins, amid bouquets of flowers. We enjoyed the leftovers immensely. The Cliveden Club booked us for a couple of years or so before the shows came to an end; maybe the members did not find our performances conventional enough, who knows?

The general public who attended were mostly Trust members and everything went well, with full houses. The difficulty in later years, once the original officer had left, was around who to deal with when setting up the weekend. One person in the estates office would readily agree the dates and mooring position, but when we arrived we could be met with a furious outburst from an official in a more senior position who knew nothing of the arrangement. This went on in a rather vague way until finally we could not continue. The stretch of riverbank and lawn where we moored was ruthlessly guarded by the National Trust, which charged high fees for mooring there. We couldn't hang on to our "free of charge" weekend any longer and the Cliveden years ended. We certainly made the best of our time there, enjoying the splendid gardens and woods, and inviting friends and family to picnics next to the barge in idyllic surroundings.

Following Cliveden, we would make the long journey to Richmond, with a feeling of relief as we arrived on our own mooring. Here there was added excitement as it is tidal on this section and the river can rise a good 20 feet on a spring tide. Sometimes we used to get caught at the end of the show when the tide was up, and the audience could not get off the pontoon. We have had to come up with all sorts of solutions, from using extra gangplanks to ferrying them off in a dinghy. Some people would take off their shoes and paddle across, something non-locals would never do! It took a few seasons to know how to time the start of performances in order to avoid the high tide.

High tide at Richmond

Richmond, just twenty minutes from the centre of London, is considered to be London's greenest borough; an eclectic mix of water meadow, flood plain, 21 miles of meandering River Thames and the world-famous Royal Park. Over time, the town has changed from being a country getaway for the royal family and court followers to become the beautiful, sophisticated place it is today. Across the river is Twickenham, the home of rugby. Other attractions include Kew Palace and Gardens, the London Wetland Centre, Ham House and Hampton Court Palace – not to mention the oldest polo club in London.

Besides tides, pubs and civilisation, the river also offers various goings-on – one such is the annual Great River Race, held in September, where rowing boats with crews of all description race upstream from the Isle of Dogs in London's East End to finish just above where the barge is moored, in Richmond, at Ham House. Every boat in the race must carry one passenger who can steer if necessary and is allowed to swap places with a rower. One year the Puppet Barge sponsored a crew to row in the race. We hired a London cutter and managed to get a crew from the Leander Club in Henley; we had five gold-medal rowers plus three others. Gren was hoping for a winning place but unfortunately the crew saw it as a bit of fun and came tenth. The race features an amazing selection of boats that varies from year to year, and has included skiffs, cutters, naval whalers, Chinese dragon boats, Hawaiian war canoes, shallops, skerries, wherries, a replica 54-foot Bronze Age Greek galley and a canvas-and-tar Irish *aomhógI* (currach), of the type reputed to have crossed the Atlantic in the eighth century. As we write, in the year 2018, the race will see American crews joining in, with boats from Australia, Bermuda, Canada, Croatia, Poland, Holland, Italy, Sweden, France, Germany, Ireland, Kuwait and the Channel Islands .

Even Punch has found himself performing for both children and adults who are waiting for the boats to cross the winning line.

The Puppet Barge crew cross the finishing line, marked by Turk's galleon

Chapter 25

Argy Bargy

I am not arguing with you – I am telling you.
James McNeill Whistler
The Gentle Art of Making Enemies (1890)

With the new millennium, the time had arrived for us to assess our situation and make sure that we were heading in the right direction. Not an easy task, but one that had to be done. After presenting shows for a number of years and trying things out, we started to question our motives for running a theatre and Gren began making notes for a blog on the web. These included questions such as: do we, the people, want a marionette theatre presenting drama that reflects the history and pulse of the society that makes up an audience? Is there an audience available, and what sort of audience do we, the presenters of marionette drama, want? In whose interest is it that we should have a marionette theatre?

The answers to these questions are complex. No doubt a professor of marionette drama would be able to articulate views that would both give us answers and at the same time refute our ideas, like a conjuror, so we would be unable to see what trickery he had used.

In this, the second decade of the 21st century, there are two marionette theatres in London, a city of some nine million or more people. The first, the Little Angel Theatre (formerly the Little Angel Marionette Theatre) has been open to the public for more than fifty years but no longer presents marionettes, despite having the staging to do so. It has seating for one hundred. The second marionette theatre is our barge, which has seating for 55. It has been open for nearly forty years and 95 percent of its performances are marionette dramas. Approximately seven thousand

An Italian marionette keeps guard

people, a mixture of adults and children from all social classes, attend a marionette performance in this theatre every year. That is 0.007 percent of the population. This audience is happy with this form of public art. From this statistic one would presume that "the people" do not want a marionette theatre, but the marionettist believes exactly the opposite.

Is it in the interest of the marionettist that we should have marionette theatres, or in the interest of the people? If the word "people" is synonymous with "society", then the question is this: is it in the interest of society that marionette drama should be supported at the same level as the actor's theatre? The answer: yes.

Such a positive answer requires explanation, but to understand completely one must be experienced with the marionette and its audience. In the first place it must be clearly understood and accepted that each and every puppet proprietor throughout the world makes and presents shows in a genre of their own.

There are three types of puppetry: marionette theatre, shadow theatre, and glove and rod puppet theatre. The marionettists are the smallest tribe, the aristocrats, while the shadow proprietors are the poets; the rod-puppet tribe – encompassing rod, glove and object theatre – will accept all comers and dominate the medium, but paradoxically require the least skill.

Exactly ten years after acquiring the barge, Gren published a broadsheet entitled *The Manipulator*. He approached John Phillips and John Wright for their views. Wright, founder of the Little Angel, sent Gren the following:

> *In the marionette I see a form of delight. Here in the combined forces of design, sculpture, drama and dance, is a joyful power, which can be communicated without recourse to any form of disguise or distortion.*

A man who can express himself through the marionette can mix with the mighty and with the poor, with old and with the young. He can appeal to the high intellect and involve his creative urge in the interests of simple people. Such is the magic of the marionette that he can speak to the deaf and communicate with disquieted minds.

After much thought and discussion with Phillips, puppeteer and intellectual, we started to get a clear idea of the power of the marionette. Although the very strings that control the movements of the figure are often quite substantial, the fascination of the marionette is in its ambiguity. It has two ways of involving its audience: first by its crafted or carved nature – in this way it becomes a caricature figure – and secondly by its lifelike properties, which evoke wonder and mystery and underline its hidden powers. In his essay for *The Manipulator*, John Phillips concluded:

As inanimate objects, the puppets produce a comic or grotesque effect. If they are perceived as living beings, then their movements produce the sensation of something wonderful, unexplainable, and enigmatic, almost magical. By seeing puppets as either comic or serious the subtle humour that the figures produce gives the appearance that they act like real people. The fact that the audience is aware that the puppets are not alive recedes, and they get the feeling that something inexplicable, enigmatic, and astounding is happening although we know very well that the figures are solid and the means of operating them are performed by living people (puppeteers).

It is the reduced size of the figures that forestalls a feeling of unease in the audience, often found in the actor's theatre. Instead a quality of serious mysteriousness is imparted. In actuality the spectator looks through the proscenium arch and focuses on the puppets as though looking into another world.

In an article for the Puppet Guild Newsletter, John Blundall, an eminent puppet master in the twentieth century, wrote:

Of all the various puppet techniques the marionette is one of the most complex requiring good design, construction, also lengthy rehearsal and general practice over a long period time. Yes, intending puppeteers, or actors looking for other options for performing, choose techniques that are easier to create and are obviously inclined to avoid the marionette. All puppet techniques require in-depth study of the body language of different types of character and their inner life and actions.

Blundall wrote in the same article about the soul of the puppet, about which we, and our company of marionettists, take a completely opposite view – as we are entitled to, after more than three decades of marionette making and presentation, unique in this country. He wrote:

One problem with the marionette can be the length of strings, particularly long ones. The soul of the puppet is in the palm of the hand, and the further the puppet is away from the hand the less life, soul and character it has.

The soul of the marionette is, in fact, transmitted through the strings that are in the hands of the operator and not through a facial expression of an operator or the simple handling required for a glove or rod puppet. Dear John, as Whistler says: "I am not arguing with you – I am telling you".

In 2009, our daughter Kate, who had been working alongside us over the years, came up with an idea that has lasted until now and hopefully will continue under her management. It is a yearly event presented on the barge in the early summer and goes under the title of "Argy Bargy"; a slang term pronounced *Ahr-jee-barjee*. The term originated in Scotland around 1600, and according to the dictionary, means "a lively disputatious discussion" or "a wrangling argument".

Many puppeteers who have trained and worked on the barge go on to make and create their own work. This includes marionette and table-top shows, film and animation. In celebration of this creativity, and to provide a platform for professional artists in the community to share new work, Argy Bargy created a unique opportunity for groups and individuals to perform and present a selection of diverse shows to an invited audience.

The event evolved after a request from a skilled puppeteer who wished to present a shadow piece, never seen before, to a supportive and critical audience who would give honest feedback and comment. It has since become a carefully planned and structured evening, which has proved highly popular with many individuals who return every year. Work has ranged from debates about death and the meaning of nothingness to explorations, using light and music, of known stories.

It is an original and ephemeral evening of creativity, which has inspired and facilitated the birth of future projects, keeping the tradition of the marionette alive and relevant for the 21st century.

Puppeteer Sarah Fitzpatrick describes one of the Argy Bargy evenings thus:

> *'Dispute' and 'argument' are words generally perceived as having negative connotations, but when it comes to creativity a heated discussion can sometimes be quite a productive means of bashing around an idea and consolidating one's own thoughts on a particular subject. The highly charged atmosphere encourages even the shyest of wallflowers to chime in with their twopenceworth. But talking is one thing; actually 'doing' is another kettle of fish altogether. It is one thing to debate the positive aspects and the flaws of somebody else's work, but quite another to thrust one's own work into the glaring spotlight of constructive criticism and weather the blows ...*

Needless to say, discussion is always livened up by a bottle or two of red or white wine and occasionally champagne or the popular stand-in, Prosecco.

At one of the Argy Bargy evenings, Gren presented a piece adapted from an interview that Howard Barker had given after a London run of *All He Fears*. A marionette scorpion plays the part of Howard and is questioned by one of the beetles:

1ST BEETLE   *(Interrupting)*   Puppetry is thought to be as much about fine art, design and movement as about verbal communication: was the process a new way of producing a text?

SCORPY   I understand the importance of fine art elements in puppetry, but this does not seem more critical than in living stage. But as for movement, yes I knew at once here was a clear distinction from stage practice, as well as in the extent to which the director/operator possesses absolute control of the creation of mood. Those constraints of speech – the puppet cannot articulate – did not seem a reason to reduce speech, however. The speech and the demonstration of movement in the body of the puppet gave precisely that detail and excess I aspire to. To speak melancholy and to express melancholy simultaneously in the body – how many actors can do that? Very few.

2ND BEETLE   How did you – do you – view the result?

SCORPY   There was much to applaud in the production. But the Movingstage Co. was learning as I was, dealing with new things, dealing with excess.

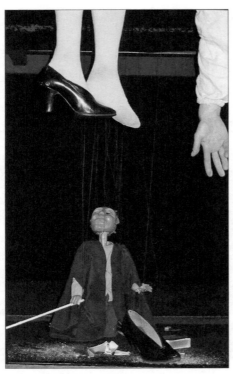

Botius confronts his girlfriend's shoe

1ST BEETLE Were your original ideas and artistic intentions reinforced or distorted by the aesthetic and the puppetry of this production?

SCORPY   The brilliance of some of their solutions amazed me – such as the massive leg that extended into the grave – hugely disproportionate to the little figure in the dark ... and the climbing of the endless rope – impossible in live theatre.

Beetles clap

It was an exhilarating journey working with Howard and a great learning process, which has stood us in good stead ever since. Sometime after presenting *All He*

Fears, Gren was able to write an essay entitled *Why Promote Text-based Drama for Live Animation,* for the *Contemporary Theatre Review* (Vol. 9, Part 4, 1999) in which he stated:

> *The reasons an artist responds to text are bound to be complex. The artist stimulated by text may be a painter, sculptor, composer or, in this modern age, one who may work in a multidisciplinary form. At the very least, the vocabulary of the writer is vast compared with what can be offered by any visual discipline not dependent on words.*

And so our choice is to work with the marionette, whose power, depth, beauty, mystery and ambiguity – if we can nurture this form of theatre and fully exploit its qualities – is able to captivate and transcend our audience. This is the challenge we have chosen, with delight.

Chapter 26
Life and Living

Since the early days, the River Thames has been a law unto itself. People used to hunt for bodies in the water, selling them on to medical establishments, while others would look for loot that had fallen in, lost by other people. It has been, and still is, a pretty hard core place on which to work. It has its own mysteries; the tidal section can be very dangerous and even big destroyer ships get carried away by the tide. There is still piracy on the waters. If you're a puppeteer, you become involved in guerrilla warfare and if, on top of that, you have a theatre on a barge, a bit of piracy is thrown in in order to stay alive.

It is not possible to make a lot of money on the Puppet Barge, because the number of seats is finite; once you are achieving full houses the only way to increase income is to raise seat prices. If seat prices are increased, income rises above the level for VAT registration; then VAT has to be charged on seats sold, which makes the profit and loss account extremely difficult to navigate.

Conditions are not bad at all if you work on a marionette stage or work with puppets; they would be the same anywhere in the world. In fact, in your own venue, it's nicer because it's more controlled. That said, it is a bit cramped on the barge and there is not enough space for luxurious green rooms in the old theatrical tradition. Facilities are limited, so one has to heave to a little bit.

The barge, MV Maybrent, with a crew of "pirates" aboard

On a barge, or on a boat of any sort, everything has to be brought on and taken off physically, including food and people. Those on board produce waste; the waste has to be removed, which is quite a process. On the tidal section of the river the sewerage can still be pumped out of the tank into the water on an outgoing tide. There is not a great volume in one pump out compared with the millions of gallons of river water passing by every hour of the day. In 1858, the year of the "great stink", the sewage, which had been draining into the river for some time, caused such a dreadful smell that lime curtains had to be hung in the House of Commons to alleviate it.

You cannot, of course, "pump out" straight into a canal and there are not many places with pumping out facilities. The canal system generally is very poorly served – once, it cost us £250 to pump out, and at one time we had to get a big tanker to carry the waste away. Nowadays there are a couple of trading boats that will come alongside and pump out the tank into a bigger tank, which is then taken to a sanitary station.

The Puppet Barge has two very small cabins under the seating rake; they resemble cells in a village police station. Each trainee will have a cabin and will enjoy a three-month experience that they won't forget.

On board, cooking is a communal affair and during a tour turns are taken by those who can cook and those who are willing to learn. The barge has a galley with a two-burner stove, an oven and hot water that serves the galley and the shower.

There's no such thing as regular leisure time during a season. There is a fixed pattern of work and company members relax between shows. For instance, in summer there is a show every day at 2.30pm, so the theatre has to be smart, tidy, clean and shipshape with all personal gear put away at least half an hour before the audience comes on board. Once the performance is finished and the audience has disembarked, everything falls apart again; the personal gear comes out and people relax. Sometimes there are jobs to be done or repairs to be made, publicity to be put out in the town or a little bit of rehearsal to be gone through.

If it's a lovely sunny day people go out on the deck and sunbathe or swim in the river, so it is quite good fun, but it also has its rhythm. The barge can be in "public" or "live-aboard" mode and both must be strictly adhered to as regards timing. A certain amount of discipline is required from all involved, proprietors and subordinates.

Trainees are asked to make a shadow show during the time they are with us; just a short show, and they can choose their own subject. Juliet helps them with making and manipulation, so by the end of the summer they have created something which is all their own work, and which may help them with the difficult decision as to whether they want to go on and become professional puppeteers. We then have an evening when everyone turns up and watches their shows, claps and gives encouragement. Some of the trainees go on to make it as puppeteers, and others don't.

Once upon a time there was a famous French pirate called La Buse – "The Buzzard" – real name Olivier Levasseur. He knew the importance of discipline. Fleeing from the authorities, he moored up in a small bay in the Seychelles hiding from both the British and French Navies.

Knowing he had to keep his crew disciplined, he conceived the most amazing plan to hide his booty. The crew were given the job of digging a tunnel that went under the sea. The pirates who had a share in the booty had to dig for a six-hour day. Gren once met a man in the Seychelles who thought he had a map of the tunnel that the pirates had dug. He spent years trying to locate the treasure and then one day he announced that he had found the spot where it was hidden. He gathered together the local press and dignitaries to witness the uncovering of the pirate treasure. It was a tragic scene; it turned out not to be there.

"The Buzzard"

Chapter 27

Rusty Times

There cannot be a crisis next week. My schedule is already full.
Henry Kissinger
The New York Times Magazine(June 1, 1969)

Millennium mischief was fast approaching, and the barge pirates began to plot and plan for the coming of the 21st century. This set our minds to work and we decided to give that well-known puppet rebel, Mr Punch, his strings back as part of the celebration. In the seventeenth century the Italians, still aggrieved that their Roman soldiers were thrown out of this country, decided to punish the English by introducing Punch to these shores – a wicked character who beats children and treats his wife shamefully. And so the old rogue arrived, complete with strings. His first review was penned by Samuel Pepys in 1662, following a performance at Covent Garden. Quintessentially Punch is now an English character, having been here some centuries. He has been banned by certain councils, but at the same time he is full of fun.

After a while the wandering puppeteers got fed up both with carting marionette staging about and dealing with badly behaved children, who were adept at interfering with Mr Punch. To bring an end to this two-pronged aggravation, the puppeteers constructed an enclosed booth and put Punch into glove form, where he remained for more than three centuries – until we had the bright idea of putting him and his cohorts back on strings.

Punch has such a bad reputation for his anarchic behaviour that people think he should be confined to the beach! It was clear to us that we would need traditional artists in the form of a writer and a maker, able to create a marionette with the character of the old rascal. We knew just the writer, Punch "Professor" Glyn Edwards, and he agreed to write us a script. Gren admitted he was not up to capturing the character of Punch in a carved marionette. By a wonderful chance he knew the man for the job, Ken Barnard, great-grandson of Richard Barnard, who had joined the company of the "Middleton Theatrical and Marionette Booth" in the nineteenth century. Richard went on to marry into the company and to tour throughout Europe.

Ken Barnard was a master artist who held the tradition of the marionette, and Punch, in his soul. It was wonderful that he was able to carve a complete set of figures for our millennium play. He and Glyn Edwards were a duo made in heaven!

Since then the Punch play, *Millennium Mischief*, has changed its name and is now *Joey's Fireworks*. Mr Punch's best friend and co-conspirator, Joey the Clown, agreed to be in the title of the show; both he and Punch are very popular and capable of attracting large audiences.

Mr and Mrs Punch and baby

In addition to the Punch play, we also managed to obtain funding from Westminster for another production celebrating the millennium. Our Rob Humphreys, father of Stanley and Joshua, wrote a half-hour play for us about ancient Westminster entitled *City Revelations*. Being the author of the *Rough Guide to London*, Rob knew London history thoroughly. This was to be our Christmas production for 1999 and into 2000 as part of the millennium celebrations.

Just before New Year 2000, we moved *Eroda* into Surrey Docks, where we were moored very close to the Greenwich Meridian Line, made visible on the opposite bank by means of a green laser beam. From here we were able to witness the grand fireworks show at the exact turn of the century. The merriment soon passed, however, and the work of presenting the two productions, which had kept us busy creatively throughout the previous winter and summer, had to be continued well into the exciting new century.

The year 2000 was both successful and enjoyable. Celebrations did not stop on January 2; three months later Natasha's son Thomas, our third grandson, was born – a millennium baby. As soon as we could we had him working on the barge and in the workshop. But as Henry Kissinger had pleaded, so did we; a full season of performances was scheduled for the summer tour. So, of course, it happened. On the annual river trip, the crisis occurred!

We were busy doing maintenance work on the interior sides of the barge while moored up at Marlow; this required rigorous rubbing down of old paintwork, getting rid of rust patches and painting. Amy Hazeldine, one of our star puppeteers and a stickler for a perfect job, had been cleaning up a section with vigour when lo and behold, she went through the 0.2 inches of iron, which had rusted, creating a small hole through which spurted a jet of water! We tried to block the hole with a wooden plug, but it did not work. Finally, Amy stood waist deep in the river holding her thumb over the hole under the water, rather like the Dutch boy on the dyke. While she did this, Gren glued a small square of hard plastic onto the inside, using a marine filler. Fortunately, this worked, and the job held out until we got to Richmond, where we arranged an emergency visit to MSO Marine at Brentford for repairs at the end of the tour.

The visit turned into a complete and utter nightmare of great proportions. Jake Oliver, boss of MSO, arranged for a surveyor to examine the barge while it was in the dry dock. The guy was a meticulous German, precise and a perfectionist! His report tore the barge to shreds and he condemned it to the scrap heap. We were both utterly shocked. Feeling extremely shaken up, we took ourselves off to the The London Apprentice, a riverside pub at Isleworth, for lunch and a place away from the yard where we could think. We sat at a table in a quiet corner contemplating the grim situation that we had suddenly found ourselves thrust into. It was so devastating we could hardly eat our lunch and the only thing we could drink was water. A double whisky might have been better.

With no solution, we made our way back to the yard to have a discussion with Jake. Neither of us could think positively, let alone know where to turn to next. Fate had struck an almighty blow and we did not know how to respond.

We arrived at the yard and were let into the main workshop, which is in a large black hangar. We were directed to the office, built on an upper platform, and, with drooping shoulders, we climbed up the iron stairs to meet with Jake, whom we had met only twice before. The office was far from salubrious. We sat down facing Jake who, at that moment, was the executioner's manager, paid to deliver the death blow to the puppet barge. His first words were, "Don't worry – I think we can make a plan". Those words were comparable to a bear finding honey!

The barge at low tide in Jake's dock

Jake then told us there were two options he could offer. He could plate or weld each rivet singly or he could cover the whole of the bottom with 0.2 inches of steel plate. He voiced the only problem that remained, "Would you be able to raise the money?"

We sat up, with shoulders back, not knowing whether to remain in a deep depression or to smile and answer in the affirmative. Very sensibly we asked for a rough quote and the rest of the day to consider the money question. Would we be able find £25,000 to pay for the repairs? By the time we had driven home the decision had been made. We would do it.

We cashed in an endowment policy, which was attached to the mortgaging of our house; this raised £17,000. Juliet then set up an appeal to everyone on the Puppet Barge mailing list, explaining our situation and asking for any donations, however small, in order to find the rest of the amount needed. This brought a wonderful response and we were able to raise the rest of the money through the generosity of the fans. To this day we love both the fans and Jake Oliver who saved the MV *Maybrent*, known as the Puppet Theatre Barge. As we write it has been open for more than 35 years, having been created in the last century. Long live the *Maybrent*! Three cheers!

The Puppet Theatre Barge after repairs

The barge has gone on to serve the company well and many hundreds of performances have been given since that time. The one disadvantage incurred by the repair is that the extra weight of steel on the hull has increased the draft of the vessel by nearly a foot. This has made it really difficult to navigate both the Grand Union and the Regent's canals, where silt has reduced the depth of the water. We now find it almost impossible to move the barge on the Paddington Arm or the Grand Union between Bull's Bridge and Brentford, for example. Recently we have travelled between Little Venice and Richmond by using the Regent's Canal up to Limehouse, then heading out on to the Thames and up to Richmond. This avoids a lot of shallow water and had become a necessity.

Chapter 28

Toe the Line

The Law is the true embodiment
Of everything that's excellent.
It has no kind of fault or flaw,
And I, my Lords, embody the Law.
W S Gilbert
Iolanthe (1882)

At some point during the year 2000, the government began to consider a change in the law for the licensing of premises used for public entertainment. Anarchy had arisen with the evolution of raves at which hundreds of young people would mysteriously appear for the evening, dancing and partying until the early hours. Management of these events was secretive, thus annoying local residents, the general grown-up public and the local councillors – who began to notice their popularity dwindling.

Other major concerns were voiced by various practitioners. Touring companies had to abide by a myriad of different regulations, as each council throughout the country had its own way of interpreting entertainments' legislation. Private clubs did not have to undergo local authority safety inspections or abide by strict time limitations; a serious event occurred in a club in Spitalfields, where a fire caused a number of deaths.

All these factors began to mount up and the government reacted. The result was the slow parliamentary process of creating an Act that would allow the control of entertainments of every sort, from musical gatherings to puppet theatre. From this began to emerge the premises licence legislation. Gren had been following the politics of licensing for some time, having escaped the necessity for a licence previously when citing the Theatres Act. Now, realising the issue could not be avoided, he wrote to Dr Kim Howells, the minister in charge of guiding the legislation through the initial stages, asking him if we would have to apply for a licence from each local authority we visited when we toured. He also wrote to Hackney MP, Diane Abbott, who responded, "I will certainly raise your concerns about the Bill when it reaches the Commons".

Some months later, the Department for Culture, Media and Sport wrote to Gren saying: "I can assure you that with regard to your barge you would only need to apply for one premises licence from the licensing authority in the area where the barge is usually moored or berthed". Perhaps his letter had some effect on the politics!

All we needed to do now was to apply for the licence. Immediately the legislation was passed we applied to Westminster Council and were assigned a council officer to handle our case. The officer was as new to the legislation as Gren, which was to our advantage, and we received plenty of help with the application. It was a huge document, approximately half-an-inch thick, and numerous copies had to be presented to different authorities, including the Coastguard, which was amusing at the time. Each authority had to respond within 28 days if they had any objections.

One major issue in our application was the need for planning permission. The barge was moored, in agreement with British Waterways, in Little Venice. This area is very exclusive and Browning's Pool was, and still is, a pearl in the authority's eye; we dreaded refusal for planning. We knew that we had been mooring in Little Venice annually for more than twelve years and, as no one had objected, could therefore qualify for permission, but we would have to prove it. We started by contacting the council planning department and were referred to the relevant officer. Gren duly introduced himself and told the officer about the barge; she responded by saying that she knew we had been in Little Venice for that amount of time as she had taken her children to a show there at least twelve years before. She duly gave us planning permission. It wasn't long before we were given our licence. Fortunately for us the Coastguard failed to object within the 28 days required, but a week or two later Captain Clive Knowles, from that very organisation, duly appeared. He presumed we were a passenger boat and demanded all sorts of alterations be made, most of which we carried out. We refused to comply with one of their demands, however, a "heel test", and on December 16, 2005, Gren wrote to the surveyor in charge at the Maritime and Coastguard Agency with our reasons:

I am writing to you in order to seek clarification of certain issues …
A premises licence has been granted to me by the Westminster City Council who have extensive experience of theatres and miscellaneous venues including boats. The Puppet Barge is a unique vessel and I submit that it should be placed in a category of its own. I am not aware of any legislation and no authority has ever intimated that the vessel should fulfil such an obligation as a "heel test".

It is my submission that the expense of conducting such a test should have been made clear at the time of my premises licence application or the British Waterways and Environment Agency licence applications and not in retrospect.

I am happy to fulfil all the improvements that Captain Knowles has requested. The vessel is always tied up when there is an audience on board and it is quite obvious that the boat is extremely stable. I surmise that the vessel does not even heel one degree with 55 persons in the audience. I submit that if your surveyor, who conducts heel tests, were to attend a public performance, he would agree with me and declare a heel test to be unnecessary. I also understand that it would be possible to commission a mathematical or computer-generated calculation of the degree of heel, certainly accurate enough for a vessel such as the Puppet Theatre Barge.

I trust you will look on my submission in the spirit in which it is made as I consider it is an infringement on our historical rights to be made to conduct a heel test on the vessel, as it is not a passenger boat. I should be able to operate the puppet barge freely in line with UK human rights legislation.

Further detail was given to the MCA in the letter. They never responded, and we have not heard from them since! Our premises licence is now framed and hanging in the entrance of the barge. It is a wonderful position to be in – fully legitimate!

Fanfare for the barge! Puppets by Dr Jack Bourne

Chapter 29

Change of Scene

Trust one who has gone through it.
Virgil *(19BC)*
Aeneid

Nancy Mitford once said, "abroad is unutterably bloody". And so it can be, but it is not always – sometimes it has its moments, and sometimes life at home can be just as bloody. Our experience of travel so far was to tour Pakistan and Palestine a number of times, with a couple of short excursions into Europe. The "bloody" aspect of touring, we estimate, makes up fifty percent of the time spent away, less if one goes on holiday, say to France – though even this can be "bloody".

Following our second tour of Palestine in 1995, Jamal Ghosheh, head of the Palestinian National Theatre, spoke to us about the possibility of sending a couple of his theatre members to England in order to learn about the marionette. On our return home, we thought about his proposition very carefully and decided, at the time, that it would not be feasible. In retrospect, we cannot decide if our reasoning was fair or not. Here is a quote from Gren's letter explaining our thinking:

Much artistic and technical experience/work must be accomplished before you turn to the marionette. It is very difficult to hold the audience's attention when a string puppet show is presented. All the elements must be in place.

The letter continued with some descriptive examples of our experience in Palestine, followed by:

While I was watching your closing ceremony I became aware of many technical problems or difficulties which I should not, as an audience member, have been made aware of. For instance, you had great problems with the length of the microphone cable, the instrument for the two musicians (who did not even play) which should have been wired up and in place before the audience entered the theatre. The wrong lights came up and it took a while for them to be corrected. All this needs hard discipline and expertise in the human theatre and even more so with the marionette theatre. I don't think it would be wise to begin with the marionette yet.

Some years later, of course, we did manage to help a Palestinian, Imad Mitwali, to make marionettes and to stage his first play. He has gone on to build a puppet theatre in a truck which tours the West Bank. We have remained in touch ever since.

There are English theatre people of the utmost sophistication who have no understanding of the marionette and should be instructed in the form before pontificating on theatre art. While attending a gathering, at which we were honouring an old director friend, there were a number of film people present including the very successful writer, David Hare. Gren managed to collar him for a minute and asked if he would consider writing a play for the marionette. Hare spurned the idea immediately, saying that he had done that as a child. Gren remembers: "His answer certainly put me in my place at the time, but since then, with a lot more experience behind me, I think he totally missed the point and had no understanding of the power of the marionette. Not that he cared!" Rejected by David Hare, we turned once more to Shakespeare, who did not reject us. We were both still eagerly trying to convince the populace, glitterati and intellectuals to take note of the power of the marionette.

In the early days, before we acquired the barge, Edward Horton, the leisure officer in our borough of Hackney, ran a policy of presenting "culture" to the people, so we could enjoy the privilege of being able to experience ballet, opera and "posh" theatre. We had been hoping to get bookings from the council when Mr Horton became aware of our existence and requested a meeting with us. We, of course, were excited at the prospect of the proposed meeting, which duly took place in the autumn of 1979. Mr Horton suggested that we make a production of selected scenes from *A Midsummer Night's Dream*.

Both of us were really keen on the idea and immediately set about reading the play. While Juliet started on an adaptation, Gren began attending lectures on Shakespeare given by all sorts of people, both actors and otherwise. There were many opportunities for extracurricular learning in the late seventies and early eighties, and Gren lapped them up like a hungry dog. He began to come up with all sorts of information about the play, including the fact that a short version was first presented at a society wedding. We soon discovered that if you combine the fairy and rustic scenes you will have a fully formed, shorter play – which is the one that was presented at the wedding. Shakespeare later developed a full version, which was presented by James Burbage at his venue, "The Theatre", that subsequently became the Globe when the whole building was moved lock, stock and barrel to the other side of the Thames.

When we met Mr Horton he was setting up a celebration surrounding Shoreditch Church, where Burbage and his sons are buried. The Theatre was situated on the spot where Holywell Lane is today. Gren, who had the task of carving the puppets, started wandering the surrounding streets. He came across Brick Lane Market, very nearby. Here he imagined walking in Shakespeare's footsteps and began to see the "rustic" characters, also known as the "rude mechanicals", in the faces of the many men who work in the market. He used these examples to carve Bottom and his cohorts. The puppets were very successful and have since been exhibited in Italy and Austria and at various times in London, including at the 1984 International Puppet Festival. After the Shoreditch festival and touring the show, entitled *Bottom's Dream*, we began to realise that the scale of the puppets was out of kilter with the large theatres and arts centres that we were playing – another reason to find a venue of our own. This led to the search for the barge and all our subsequent adventures.

Following the success of *Bottom's Dream* and the acquisition of the barge, it was some years before we started on our next Shakespeare production. But our first attempt had given us not only the confidence but also a hunger to experience more of Shakespeare's exquisite poetry, teamed up with our handmade characters. We couldn't resist it. In 1987, we chose to stage *The Tempest*. Not only did it have magic, it also had a storm and a floundering ship, which we thought would be highly relevant to the barge.

"Say the bells of Shoreditch"; the display outside the church

The style of the puppets we were making had moved on since *Bottom's Dream*, becoming more abstract, which suited *The Tempest* well. The faces were less naturalistic, and expressions could alter as heads turned and shadows were created.

One of the stage directions in the script reads: "Enter Ariel, invisible". This poses a problem for any production. How is it possible to bring this about? Often by dressing the actor in shiny silver paint or a black catsuit, or by presenting them as a shadowy figure, barely seen. We, however, decided to make a glass Ariel.

Prospero, carved by Gren; deep eye sockets and strong planes catch light and shadow.

John Kaye, a glassblower (found in the *Yellow Pages*), who spent most of his time making test tubes and bell jars, agreed to try and blow our Ariel for us. His studio was in Islington and we took along our Puck figure from *Bottom's Dream* as a model. John was dubious at first but warmed to the job over the weeks as we expressed our delight and enthusiasm. Certain details were tricky but between us, with John's expertise and our marionette knowledge, we created joints to allow for articulation, using tiny glass tubes which could carry nylon thread to join body parts. The final result was a transparent flying figure of clear glass, catching the light as it flew through a beam or becoming almost invisible when hidden in the shade. Our Caliban was a dark brown, naked figure, slightly hunchbacked, based on an old Italian marionette that once belonged to Gordon Craig and had been given to us by his son, Teddy. It took us approximately two years to make and stage the play which opened, on the barge, at Kingston Festival in May 1987.

Ken Griffith recorded Prospero in India, where he was filming at the time, so the quarter-inch voice tape had to be flown back to the UK for editing. In those days sound editing was laborious and time-consuming. We transferred the tapes piece by piece to a four-track mixer (known as a Portastudio) and assembled them with effects and music. It took hours and hours. However, the upside of this work is that by the time it is complete, one knows the play intimately and every line is familiar, which is exactly what is required to achieve the total synchronisation of speech and gesture; the puppet lives. It is a most creative and enjoyable process.

The start of the play was a strong moment: in darkness, with a mighty clap of thunder and flashes of lightning through which the puppeteers were glimpsed grappling with ropes and sails above the stage as the storm raged. The marionette is the perfect vehicle with which to create the "strange shapes" of the islanders and the "visions" conjured up by Prospero for the young lovers. And possibly best of all are the fearful hell-raising demons Prospero creates to punish Trinculo and Stephano. Good fun for puppeteers. *The Tempest* remains firmly in the repertoire and is well received when we present it.

To have come to know the play so well is a privilege and a joy. Maybe it is the theatre-makers and performers who get the most delight and satisfaction from such work; the audience enjoy it (we hope) but the workers fly.

Caliban, Antonio and Sebastian

… cynicism is left at the door and we are able to delight in a rare magical experience not often afforded to adult eyes.

Coco Hall, *Remotegoat* website, November 13, 2010

We re-presented *The Tempest* several times, including in 2010. It is always nice to boast of excellent reviews and it is encouraging to know that people like one's work. It drives a person to do even more, and so it was that we eventually tackled our third Shakespeare play. And what an experience that was.

We chose *Macbeth,* his shortest play, but one with an abundance of magic and drama. Juliet adapted the script. The depth of the language and the opportunities to explore ways of presenting the surreal scenes was thrilling. The witches were airborne; a huge dagger fell from above, quivering as its point stuck into the stage; Banquo's ghost was made in glass and Birnam Wood strode on stilts to Dunsinane.

At the time, we had let out one of our rooms to an Australian artist, Lucy Turner, whose work we enjoyed. She also had some knowledge of puppets, so we commissioned her to make them, to our specifications, although she was responsible for final design. Our actors were very carefully chosen, and we were lucky to obtain the services of people at the top of their profession such as Roger Lloyd-Pack, Peter Reeves, Gillian Barge and, in the lead part, Toby Stephens, the talented son of Maggie Smith and the late, great Robert Stephens.

Coincidentally, in 1999 and 2000, the years we presented *Macbeth,* there was a surfeit of production companies staging the play. Corin Redgrave was in the lead at Battersea Arts Centre, directed by Tom Morris, later of *War Horse* fame. There was also a production at the Cochrane Theatre, an African production at Ovalhouse and an RSC show at the Young Vic, so competition was fierce.

To be reviewed alongside the big theatre companies was heartening. In *The Times,* Ian Michaels had this to say, *A fine addition to Movingstage's repertoire; this* Macbeth *displays a scale of ambition that proves these puppeteers can also think big.* Meanwhile, *What's On* editor and critic Oliver Jones wrote, ... *the skill of the marionettists must be mentioned by name.*

We agree: the marionettists who worked on the London run were Juliet, Kate, Jonathan Broughton, Sue Dacre and Lynn Robertson-Bruce; Rachel Leonard was with us on the Thames tour. As always it was a thoroughly enjoyable and enlightening experience getting so close to Shakespeare; the very opposite to learning about him at school.

Since that time our Lady Macbeth has had a change of costume and has played other parts on a couple of occasions. Hopefully she will return to her original role one day and the production will be re-presented to a new audience. Not long before we presented *Macbeth,* primary schools had begun teaching Shakespeare to the top three years, so theatregoers will be up to scratch when watching a Shakespeare production now.

Kenneth Tynan, the theatre critic, once visited Gordon Craig when he was living in Italy. During the interview Craig, whose mother, Ellen Terry, had played Lady Macbeth and whose portrait hangs in the National Portrait Gallery, said to Kenneth, "I'm beginning to solve the problem of staging the cauldron scene in *Macbeth.* I'm not certain yet, mind you, but it's getting clearer. It's getting clearer every day ..." Suddenly, "Did you ever think that Shakespeare had a cat? Look at the sonnets. Most of them aren't written to a woman or a boy. They are addressed to a cat."

Macbeth and Lady Macbeth, carved by Lucy Turner

We had become custodians of some of Gordon Craig's figures, including several marionettes, given to us by Teddy, his son. We have them displayed in our home in Hackney. Gordon Craig came back into our lives in 2013, when Nenagh Watson, intellectual and former puppeteer, approached us with a request to use our Craig puppets for an exhibition entitled *Dead Puppet*. The show was also going to feature puppets from Nenagh's previous company, Doo-Cot, which had had a formidable reputation in the 1990s and early 2000s. Nenagh had tutored our grandson Stan at the Central School of Speech and Drama and roped him in to help set up the exhibition, which was first mounted in Manchester.

Nenagh liked seeing the puppets in the domestic environment of our home. She said that this added to the notion of a "living archive" and to the poignancy of these fragile figures. Following the exhibition, she went on to organise a gathering of puppet aficionados and intellectuals on the barge, in order to prove that the twelve puppets once owned by Craig and given to us by his son were what we claimed they were. The puppet intellectuals wanted positive proof that the puppets had been part of Craig's collection.

International experts Paolo Parmigiana, archivist and researcher at the Museo Giordano Ferrari o Castello dei Burattini in Parma; John McCormick, scholar from Trinity College Dublin; and Michael Dixon, archivist for the British Puppet and Model Theatre Guild, were invited to take part. Nenagh named the event *A Creative Banter*.

In order to gain funding for the "banter", and to really appreciate Craig's writing for puppets, we decided that a short piece inspired by his texts would help persuade funders to fund. To this end we presented a living-room version of Craig's *The Tune the Old Cow Died of*. Many years before, John Wright had presented the piece at the Little Angel as an interlude alongside *Soldier's Tale*. At that time Simon Rattle played the typewriter and Gren did the lighting.

The experts at *Creative Banter* were seeing the puppets for the first time. The audience watched as the exhibits were examined, and enjoyed much excitement – and indeed banter – as to their origin. They were able to see fine details of the figures as each piece was photographed and projected onto a screen.

The body and other parts from Gordon Craig's suitcase given to us by his son

We are happy to say that after much discussion and investigation of the puppets; the experts did verify them as the genuine article. The discovery of a tiny initial carved on the sole of a puppet foot, identifying a carver who worked for Craig, was a thrilling moment. Since then they have been exhibited at the Gordon Craig Theatre in Stevenage but still have their permanent base with us. As far as we know it is doubtful whether the citizens of Stevenage have any idea who Craig was, despite their theatre being named after him.

The Mayor of Stevenage operates one of the Craig puppets, amusing the curator of the exhibition.

Chapter 30

Ambition

There must be a beginning of any great matter, but
the continuing unto the end until it is thoroughly
finished yields the true glory.
Francis Drake *1540-96*
Dispatch to Sir Francis Walsingham (May 17, 1587)

Following the experience of presenting three of Shakespeare's plays, our knowledge of life and of the marionette had taken a huge leap forward. We both concluded, as theatre makers might, that imagination is the master of art and of life. Our minds were buzzing furiously.

As it happened, fate dictated at that time that the government, was offering Arts Council grants for work with African content. Having been born in Africa, Gren set about using his imagination. He remembered that the epigram heading T S Eliot's original manuscript of *The Wasteland* was a quote from Conrad's *Heart of Darkness*:

Did he live his life again in every detail of desire, temptation, and
surrender during that supreme moment of complete knowledge?

He cried in a whisper at some image, at some vision – he cried out
twice, a cry that was no more than a breath –

"The horror! The horror!"

It is this quote that gave birth to the idea for a marionette drama set in Africa. What better than a production entitled *Out of the Heart of Darkness?* And with Gren's years of experience in Africa the production became a possibility.

The process was helped by Becky Smith, formerly of the Puppet Centre and now running a school of puppetry in Brighton, who managed our application to the Arts Council. We received an award of £10,000 for the making of the production, a wonderful boost that enabled us to devote much of our time to creating the spectacle and employing some great actors and artists. Elizabeth Barron had trained and worked with us for a number of years, during which time we came to know that she was a talented painter as well as a skilled marionettist. We approached her to paint a set of backdrops for the play, knowing she understood the style required. She agreed, despite having to adapt to a canvas approximately 10 feet by 6 feet and to using scenic paint instead of watercolour! The results were exciting: hot sands, dark Congo jungle and riverside, complemented by Gren's atmospheric lighting.

We set about the project with enthusiasm, delving into the deepest information on the history of the Congo, Conrad, Roger Casement, Leopold II of Belgium and Mrs Mobutu. We trawled the internet making use of a wealth of facts and fiction. Both the Congo and the world of Kurtz, the novel's mysterious central figure, were an impenetrable darkness as explored by Conrad. Mobutu, the former president of Zaire, stole $6.5 billion as well as chartering Concorde to fly him from his pink palace to his dentist in France. The script was influenced not only by the diaries of Conrad and the writings of Roger Casement, but also by the works of Chinua Achebe, Carl Jung, John Coetzee, Mark Twain, William Golding and many others who have travelled to and lived in Africa.

The production took three years to adapt and construct; coincidentally it arrived on the stage at a time when Africa was at the forefront of world politics. As with the film *Apocalypse Now*, this version was freely adapted and set in the present day. Instead of ivory, illegal diamonds were the prize, and a contribution to the plot also came in the form of a real-life scam email doing the rounds that purported to come from one Mrs Mobutu, claiming to be the widow of the ex-dictator. We found a website dedicated to this email that was useful in developing the plot.

Kurtz and dancers

We were especially happy to be lauded by *The Stage,* the weekly paper devoted to theatre:

This adult production is yet another fruit of a 30-year artistic collaboration between author-designer Middleton, a former lighting cameraman, and the gifted puppeteer and costume maker Juliet Rogers, a thrilling example of their unique "live animation" technique.

While presenting the show at the end of the summer tour, moored at Richmond, we had a phone call from a woman called Susan Harcourt who told us that she wanted to bring someone very special to a show. It turned out to be Ian Player, the man responsible for saving the white rhino. Gren knew about Ian, as his old boss in South Africa had made a number of films with the charismatic big game expert and conservationist. Coincidentally Gren also knew Ian's brother, Gary Player, the world-class golfer with whom he had been at school in the 1950s.

It was an honour to meet Ian and to have him see a performance. We also met Susan who acted as Ian's secretary when he was in England and had seen the show in Marlow. After the performance, Ian insisted on taking us for a coffee and we were happy to guide him to a restaurant, a few hundred yards up the towpath, facing the river. It was a most interesting evening.

Ian told us how he particularly liked the moment in the play when Conrad, in his tent at night, murmurs to himself, "We live, as we dream, alone … we search for the particles of truth, floating in a sea of insignificance". He explained how he was interested in Jung, especially his writing on dreams. We also discovered that Ian had written his autobiography and, almost in the same breath, Gren, stimulated by the success of the evening, asked him if we could make a show based on his story and managed to get his permission.

It took a year or two before we started adapting the book; we later named our production *Footprints in the Wilderness.* Gren took on the task of the writing, focusing the script on Ian's "getting of wisdom" from Magqubu Ntombela, the Zulu game warden who worked with him in Natal and who taught him so much about the natural world. Ian's voice comes through clearly as he makes the case for humanity's co-operation and positive action in the struggle to conserve wildlife and wilderness.

It ends with lines taken from *Inversnaid*, a poem by Gerard Manley Hopkins:

What would the world be, once bereft
Of wet and of wildness? Let them be left,
O let them be left, wildness and wet;
Long live the weeds and the wilderness yet.

Before finalising the making and recording of the piece, we went to South Africa to see Gren's sister and brother-in-law in Johannesburg. After a wonderful trip with them to the Kgalagadi game reserve, we set off on our own to visit Ian, on his farm, high in the hills above Natal's coastal region. He and his wife Anne lived in a traditional old bungalow surrounded by trees, birds, monkeys and luscious greenery. We had sent the script on ahead to Ian's secretary and had planned the trip in order to hear his frank comments, his requests for cuts, additions and alterations, and lastly, most hopefully, his approval of the work and permission to proceed. We were in a state of nervous anticipation as Ian poured whiskys for us all and we sat before a huge log fire that he had laid on that damp and misty mountain evening. Before very long we realised that in fact, being such a busy and sought-after man, Ian had not yet glanced at the script or even opened it! He sweetly told us to enjoy our drinks and relax while he read it. We crept away and examined treasures around the house – including a beautiful clock, similar to an orrery. When we were summoned back, Ian said with some emotion in his voice, "I couldn't ask for better". What a moment. We could now sail forth with his blessing.

After dinner we discussed the difficult path ahead and Ian's dedication to preserving wilderness and wild places around the globe. He promised to come and see the show, although by then his health was not so good.

Back home we set about the making in earnest. Juliet had written a sequence, including the creation myth of the Bushmen, which was to be presented with shadow puppets, so Colleen, with her special skills and African background, came from Scotland to help. Among other things she made a praying mantis in wire, which had a powerful aura about it.

Bushman and Elephant

Bushman in a ceremony with Mantis

The script includes scenes in the wild with Magqubu and a visit to a regimental gathering in Wales where Magqubu asks for peace for the spirits of the dead Zulu warriors and the Welsh soldiers who died at Isandlwana, and peace between the two nations forever. One of the final scenes is a philosophical conversation between an elephant and a rhino as they discuss the chances of survival in view of the callous and shortsighted behaviour of the human species. Elephant speaks:

> *Unless mankind takes note of what we say and our ways, and saves large areas of wilderness, they will surely make us and themselves extinct*

We had great support from Susie Harcourt, Jo Roberts, the CEO of the Wilderness Foundation, Lucia van der Post and Louise Aspinall. The show opened in Henley in July 2007 and moved on downriver through Marlow to Richmond, where we had two special performances for the Wilderness Foundation and one for Save the Rhino. All three were memorable evenings, attended by generous members and many special people. We drank champagne and toasted the future of the organisations and the success of the show. The crowning glory of these evenings was the presence of Ian himself, who spoke wonderfully before the performances and gave his unforgettable imitation of the cry of the fish eagle. Later, when we had a quiet moment, he gave us a cheque for £500 towards the production expenses.

Magqubu, Ian Player's assistant, addresses Welsh Regimental dinner

The year we presented *Footprints in the Wilderness* was the last year of touring the upper Thames. After much thought and careful calculations, we came to the conclusion that the figures did not balance. Sadly, the expenses incurred in licensing the boats to travel above Teddington and onto Environmental Agency waters, plus the mooring fees demanded by some local authorities, made it impossible to justify travelling above Richmond. Added to this we now had a secure mooring in Richmond where we could decide on the length of the season and so remain there for as many weeks as we chose. We felt sad to be leaving the upper Thames, which we had enjoyed for so many years, but it was the right decision. Apart from leaving us financially better off, it was not such hard work. The roof only had to be lowered and raised twice, instead of five or six times, as had been the case when moving from one mooring to another through the summer.

Chapter 31

Partition

A man travels the world in search of what he needs and returns home to find it
George Moore *1888-1923*
The Brook Kerith (1881)

When, in 2005, we received another invitation from Rafi Peer Theatre to attend its arts festival in Lahore, we had to do some serious thinking. This would be our third visit to Pakistan and we were delighted that our old friend Faizan Peerzada had contacted us.

However, it is never easy to travel anywhere with more than 25 marionettes and accompanying props, special effects, gauzes, backcloths and the like, let alone for 8000 miles. The barge would have to be closed for several weeks, and the administration of the business covered during our absence. Once we had decided we would make the trip, we asked Athena Maschi, a talented young puppeteer who had recently trained with us, to join us. Athena's French boyfriend at the time was against her going, and consequently they parted company.

The two months before we left were taken up with arrangements, bargaining, negotiations and bureaucracy between ourselves, the host company, the British Council and the Pakistan High Commission. Finally a deal was struck, but not until the eleventh hour and we needed nerves of steel to sit out the last few days. Thank goodness for emails. At least communications are swift and sure nowadays, even if language can be a bit ambiguous.

In 1992, during our second visit to Pakistan, the festival was dedicated to puppetry. Now, ten years on, the Peerzada family had expanded and developed its artistic field and for the past eight years the festival had promoted theatre, puppetry, music and dance. Puppetry was given the same status as the other art forms.

Our first three days on site were spent constructing a double-bridge marionette stage with, as on our previous visits, materials and help provided. The venue was a large stripy tent, seating about three hundred, with a stage at one end. There were seven of these tents altogether, set up around a circular structure that had two indoor theatre spaces, offices and a central arena for big concerts each night.

The arena with dancers in the foreground welcoming the audience

Making the stage was a sweaty business. The temperature rose to the mid-30s centigrade during the day but dropped as soon as darkness fell at about 6.30pm. The materials arrived; many lengths of rough timber and a bag of three-inch nails. Fortunately, we had two carpenters assigned to us who were willing and flexible. They had no power tools.

The day of our first performance was full of agitation and frustration. Lighting and sound were to be provided but just did not materialise. Two hours before the show we had some lamps in place, but it was not possible to trim them accurately onto the stage, focus or spot them up or down. The floods were better, lying on the floor with coloured gel laid on top, but the gels kept frizzling up into little balls: there were no gel holders or barn doors. The house was packed, and a sofa had been placed in the centre of the front row for the main sponsor of the festival. At the last minute, the sound gear arrived. The show goes on, it is wonderfully received ... spontaneous clapping throughout and a crowd of enthusiasts staying behind to smile, nod and handle the puppets.

The third double-bridge stage

The frustrations of the day melted away and we realised that there are small compromises and adaptations to make in order to communicate with people and make this important cultural exchange at a time of unease and conflict between the West and the Islamic world. When not performing, the three of us had time to see other shows and talk to other performers. Athena was a great asset with her youthful energy and curiosity, never having experienced the sub- continent before. After a hard day she would stay up far into the night watching shows and listening to music and making friends. Faizaan bought an entire flower stall of blooms which were delivered to her room. After several years working with Movingstage, Athena created her own theatre, with her partner Cesare Maschi, in an old London Routemaster bus; it is now one of the capital's special attractions.

Since that visit we have not ventured back to Pakistan, in spite of invitations, because of the increased tensions and unrest. The Peerzadas have had to restrict their events and have not been able to run a festival every year. More sadly, our friend Faizaan, the main organiser of the festivals, died suddenly some years after this visit. We met him as a young man, introduced to us by Penny Francis, at the Puppet Centre at the time,

Athena and Juliet with guide and army bodyguards

and it was she who told us of his death. A long and enduring friendship rewarded us with much knowledge and understanding. Faizaan used to tell us that we had introduced the marionette to Pakistan.

We had the pleasure of seeing the Peerzadas develop and promote the arts in their country, particularly puppetry. Hopefully they will be able to continue to foster peace and harmony between the Islamic world and the West through the arts, which has always been their vision. Rafi Peer was the father of this talented family, a playwright and intellectual who had lived in Berlin in the 1930s and had left, with the rise of Nazism before World War II, to return to India. Here he wrote for All India Radio and his plays were broadcast widely. Faizaan, his son, told us how people would gather in the cafés to hear the next instalment of his dramas, so popular did they become. With Partition, after the war, the Peerzada family had to leave India and go north to Lahore where they made their home.

We have travelled to both India and Pakistan, taking our shows and sometimes seeing the work of local puppeteers. After our third visit

A Punjab puppet show in action

to Pakistan, we were presented with an opportunity to visit India in a working capacity; it also offered a rare insight into local life at its least comfortable level. This came about through one of our regular audience members, Smita Biswas.

Fortunately, with good help via the internet, website and online booking, our audiences are generally on the healthy side for most shows and have become more diverse. The matinees are nearly always full, and our regulars return often.

Smita and her son Milan had attended many of our shows. One day, following a performance on the barge, she asked if we might consider visiting Kolkata to perform for the children there. She explained that her mother ran a teacher's centre, training students in the Montessori method, and also a school. The children attending were poor, orphaned or the children of prostitutes; they worked in the day and lived on the street.

It took about two years to get this project off the ground, but in autumn 2010, following a summer in Richmond, we had a definite plan. We were to go to Kolkata around mid-November and return home in early December. After our work there, we planned a trip to Darjeeling, which

Street children gathered together for the show

Juliet had always wanted to visit. She was already a tea specialist when Simon Callow came to record the voice of Scrooge for our production of *A Christmas Carol*; when asked would he like tea or coffee, he replied, "Darjeeling, darling". That did it; a visit was essential, especially as we could travel up the mountains by single-gauge "toy" railway.

About four weeks before we were due to leave, our grandson Stan contacted us one evening, saying that he had not got the university place he wanted so he was taking a year out and could he come with us. We agreed immediately.

The whole trip was made easier and more enjoyable having Stan with us. He looked after the luggage and found the correct gates for flights or platforms for trains. He darted about picking up vital things such as water or tickets, while we stood guard over the puppet boxes and our personal bags. As for the show, it improved at once having a third operator involved and became more daring and inventive, as Stan insisted on a strict rehearsal schedule with some re-working. Gren's weak protests were overruled.

Once in Kolkata, we were guests in Smita's home and were looked after well. We had our own unit and were invited to share excellent meals with the family. We worked in the school, giving shows for both the children and the student teachers. In between shows we had time to explore Kolkata and visited the Victoria Memorial museum and gardens, full of interesting history, paintings and models of battles. Victoria's statue still looks down benignly on the gardens; strange that she still survives. But so do many other features of British colonial rule. New Market, for example, is a most amazing place, a great British-built Covent Garden-type structure, completely falling down but still buzzing with full-on trading. Masses of stalls sell good vegetables and fruit, meat, live goats and chickens, fish and even cheeses. Old signs, such as "Johnson and Sons. Best Butter and Cream", still remain. We managed a ferry trip across the Hooghly River, fast-flowing and packed with craft, to visit Howrah railway station, an impressive building.

Kolkata is a marvellous city, teeming with people, many of whom are desperately poor and live on the streets. The architecture of the past is still there, often very decrepit but handsome and nostalgic. Above all it is a friendly place, moving at a slower pace than the other major Indian cities, and we never felt threatened or afraid when in among the bustling mobs. People were ready to help or direct us, although often a so-called "guide" would latch onto us and there would be no way we could disentangle ourselves until we'd given a healthy handout.

One night, after a show, Smita and her husband took us to the Tollygunge Club for dinner. It was an unbelievable jump back into the past; it could have been a film set. The club is next to a racecourse and polo field, and everything about it is as it must have been in the days of the Raj, complete with huge leather armchairs, verandahs, brass fittings and period lighting.

Our last week in India was spent travelling to and enjoying Darjeeling. We took an overnight train to New Jalpaiguri, then a truck to Kurseong, where we caught the "toy" train, a vintage steam train on a narrow gauge, up the mountains. We arrived in Darjeeling quite late at night.

It was very cold; we had climbed a few thousand feet and the temperature had dropped to near freezing. On arriving at our hotel, we

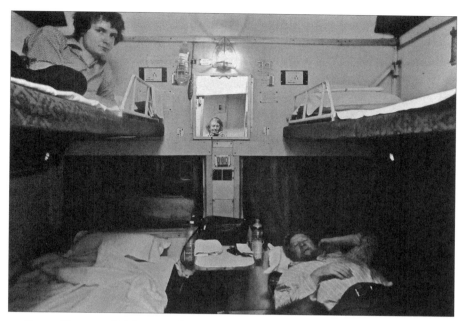

Stan, Gren and Juliet on the overnight train bound for New Jalpaiguri

were shown up some outside steps to our ice-cold bedrooms, where we climbed into the beds, covered ourselves with every bit of bedding and ordered a bottle of whisky – no food being available at that hour. The hotel seemed empty apart from us and we noticed several rolled-up shapes in passageways and under stairs, indicating that the staff had turned in.

The next few days were spent exploring the local club and library, talking to traders in the streets, visiting the zoo and lastly spending a day in the "Happy Valley" tea plantation estate. Here we were shown the whole tea production process, from picking to packing, and sampled a cup of first flush Darjeeling tea. How "happy" the valley really is is another matter. The workers live in compounds with their families, but wages are extremely low. Once in the job it is almost impossible to change course and children follow parents into the business. The growth of the industry in this area is falling off as competition increases from other regions, so the outlook for these workers is grim.

Heading back down to the hot plains below again by steam train, puffing through small towns and villages, passing monasteries with prayer flags fluttering, we descended to Kolkata and our comfortable quarters once more. Stan was planning to tour India the following year with a production of *The Red Balloon* that he and Soledad, a former trainee, were making, so before we left we managed to organise a couple of shows at the school and accommodation for their stay with Smita. The trip was a good rehearsal for Stan: using Indian railways, moving puppets and staging about, bargaining, eating out and many other aspects were handled more easily the next time round.

Darjeeling tea tasters Gren, Stan and Juliet

Chapter 32

Mind and Matter

Studies serve for delight, for ornament, and for ability.
Francis Bacon *1561-1626*
Essays 1625

In 2017, an elected Welsh MP from Monmouth, Mr David Davies, an educated man, announced in a speech that the government "... should be looking into the way that Brexit is being taught at the moment in universities – in fact, we should be looking at the way everything is being taught in universities. We are sending 50 percent of our students, young people, off to university often doing ludicrous degrees in puppetry, surf studies or media studies."

That is the sort of prejudice the puppet fraternity has suffered since the end of the nineteenth century and the man who said it must be a puppet himself, and resents the fact. (This MP is not to be confused with David Davis, the former Brexit minister.)

What Mr Davies does not understand is that puppetry is used in all sorts of ways to both educate and entertain children and adults. It has often been seen as a medium reserved for children, but modern adults are beginning to realise that a puppet show offers content that cannot be conveyed by ordinary theatre. In a puppet show pigs can talk as well as fly!

We have been presenting puppet drama for more than three decades, during which time we have learned about the power of the marionette and other puppet forms. We've produced a number of shows, many based on published works, from *The Butterfly's Evil Spell* by Federico García Lorca to Byron's *Manfred*. This experience has given us the knowledge and insight to produce our own original plays. Having acquired a degree in puppetry in the first place would have helped enormously and saved a lot of time and trouble! Our puppet adventure has also kept at least three people employed on a living wage for more than thirty years, so put that in your hat and eat it, Mr Davies.

Gren picks up here on the theme of writing and presenting of our own original texts:

"Following the productions that used classic texts, as well as the original plays that we commissioned, we felt able and strong enough to produce our own works using personal experience, outside influences and original thought. This takes courage and time, but having the opportunity to create and present one's own work is a privilege not available to many people and must be grabbed.

In early 1974, I was engaged to film a documentary about Napoleon's last days on the island of St Helena. I was introduced to the director, Mike Pearce, who had recently returned from Australia. Mike (who later made the Zakynthos film with me) had directed a film called *The Money Game*, which had been conceived and written by the Australian cartoonist and filmmaker Bruce Petty and had won various awards. It was a year or two after returning from St Helena that I was able to see the film, which features a large Heath Robinson-type machine at which various characters play the money game. The image of this machine was burned onto my mind and has stayed with me ever since. There was no hint of puppetry in the film – or in my mind at that time.

Some thirty years later, following the influence of our experience with Ian Player, I conceived the idea of producing a marionette drama that would be based on the getting of wisdom. The idea grew out of the experience of making and presenting *Out of the Heart of Darkness* and *Footprints in the Wilderness*. I set about the serious work of developing this project in 2007, starting with the questions: 'What is wisdom?' and 'How does one acquire wisdom?' After some weeks, I began to focus on just what a controlling factor money is in our lives, and how Bruce Petty had described it very well in his film. I immediately wrote to Bruce and asked permission to use the basis of his idea in a marionette drama. Happily, he agreed.

We started to put the script together, adapting some seminal experiences I have had during my years of filming. It was fun doing the research and digging into my memory.

The script slowly took shape, with the inclusion of many influences – starting with the experience of facing my school headmaster in his office. We also drew on an unforgettable visit to Zululand where the Battle of Isandlwana took place during the Zulu War. We were taken around the battleground and given the full story of the manoeuvres. The

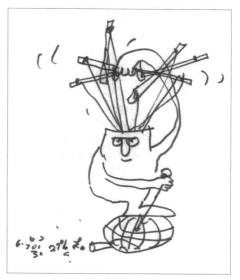

Bruce Petty cartoon drawn on the barge

area is covered with hundreds of stone cairns under each of which six British soldiers are buried. There is also a small hill, or 'koppie', where a British soldier by the name of Younghusband commanded a platoon of soldiers who fought to the death of them all.

The hero of the piece, Tom Wrigley, is taught first about war as he visits an old soldier, inspired by Younghusband, and then about peace and spiritual harmony by a boy soldier. He learns to respect life and nature from the Hopi Indians, watching them dance and hearing their philosophy on how to live in harmony with the world around. This was derived from my experience filming a documentary about the Hopi on their reservation in Arizona, where we stayed for several weeks.

The sequence of planting an acorn, with its metaphor of providing the shade and glory of an oak tree for future generations, came out of a film about Cecil Rhodes that I worked on in South Africa and England."

Tom journeys through all these encounters before he finally attends the World Series of the Money Game, which takes place annually in New York. This is where Bruce Petty's idea comes into play. Having thought of incorporating the subject of money we knew that we would have to present a smaller version of the machine for our stage. To this end we engaged the services of a former trainee, Beatrice Pentney, to make the machine. On her website, she had a picture of a mechanical presentation she created for her final show at university. She agreed to the job and the result filled our stage.

So, Tom finally attends the Money Game, visits Africa, gives his girl a conflict diamond (is it glass or the real thing? Does it matter?) and sets up a centre for war orphans with her. He learns about money, its power and perhaps how to use it wisely. We had the privilege of working with some wonderful actors on the show, including Roger Lloyd-Pack and Peter Reeves who recorded the various voice parts.

A group of The Money Game cast

The production, staged in 2011, was a great success and played at the bi-annual Suspense Festival. Created by the Little Angel Theatre under Peter Glanville, who has now moved on to the Polka Theatre, sadly the festival is no more.

Having put ourselves through the epic journey of Tom Wrigley's search for wisdom, Juliet's thoughts turned towards the young, with an original story that she conceived and wrote herself.

Beatrice Pentney's Money Machine

Chapter 33

Fowl Play

A little inaccuracy sometimes saves tons of explanation.
Saki *(H H Munro)*
The Square Egg (1924)

When programming a season of work for the barge, we would try not to re-present a production within four years of its first outing. The more shows we made the easier this became and during the first twenty years or so we made one every year. In the first decade of the 21st century, it so happened that we only produced new work for our adult audiences. This was not particularly intentional, but the inspirational moments and ideas that flowed along at the time just pushed us that way.

By the time we had created three new evening productions, we realised that there was a pressing need for a new family show and a germ of an idea had presented itself. Fate played its hand during the summer season of 2013 in Richmond, when a showbiz agent approached us out of the blue, looking for an outlet for Muffin the Mule. Muffin, a string puppet, had acquired a certain amount of fame, as he had appeared on the first ever TV broadcast made by the BBC. That was in 1936. Since then he has had nearly 200,000 views on YouTube as well as many outings with Ronnie Le Drew, the current chairman of the British Puppet and Model Theatre Guild. Originally made and directed by Jan Bussell, Muffin is now being looked after by his grandson who has finally cottoned on to his fame!

The agent wanted suggestions as to how he could forward Muffin's career. We set to and produced a synopsis of a story we thought could be made into a touring show. We were to write the script and make a version that would feature Muffin. The agent was not easy to work with so, after careful consideration, we decided that we did not want the restrictions that this would impose on us and politely declined the offer. However, we were left pondering over a mule in terms of storylines. Gren then suggested we might make a marionette play with a mule as a central character, and Juliet took on the task.

The script of *Fowl Play* went through a good few drafts before settling down, but the main theme was set around mules being different and how difference can be special. A mule is born and grows up on a farm with other animals, all of whom speak. They tease Mule because he is different, but he has special talents, in particular, tap dancing. One night, "fowl" play takes place and he is stolen: all the animals try to find him and bring him back. Adventures ensue and finally Mule is rescued. To celebrate his return a talent contest is held in which all the animals perform tricks. No prize for guessing the winner.

There was a large cast to make and assemble. Gren, in spite of protests, was instructed to carve two mules, one a foal and the other a bigger, dancing mule, each representing the character at different stages in the story.

Sarah Fitzpatrick (who had learned to carve while working with us and become very proficient) and Juliet took on pigs, chickens, cats and dogs, and Juliet also made a travelling shadow sequence depicting Mule's escape. While the carving was underway, we gathered together our actors for voice recordings and began to think about the music. Juliet had asked Matthew Scott (who had composed scores for the two Barker plays plus two other productions) if he would take it on, and he agreed. Some weeks later, Matthew contacted us to

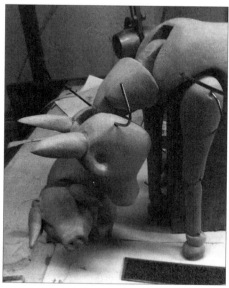

Mule and Pig under construction

say he was afraid he just wasn't able to find the time to write the music. By now he had become head of music at the National Theatre! This was February 2015 and a bad moment, as the show was scheduled to open in early May.

Sarah Fitzpatrick with Mule in his finery

Making the soundtrack, mixing and editing all the voices, music and effects takes time and can't be rushed. We had some good friends in Andrew Rankin, the drummer with the Pogues, who had recorded some wonderful percussion tracks for our *Macbeth*, and his partner Jane Perrott who interviewed us for her oral history project. Juliet phoned Jane when this crisis came upon us and Jane said immediately, "You need Stephen". She gave us contact details and we were pretty overwhelmed to discover that "Stephen" – Stephen Warbeck – was an Oscar winner for *Shakespeare in Love* and had written scores for countless plays and films to great acclaim. Juliet wrote a simple email, introducing our work and saying what we required and how much we could pay. A reply came back at once offering to write the music and suggesting we should meet soon. We were thrilled. Stephen was a pleasure to work with. He wrote a great score with animal signatures, atmospheric farmyard and adventure pieces, music for the escape back home and tap dance music; it added hugely to the success of the show. Juliet went to the studio and sat in on the live session, which was recorded acoustically on fiddle, clarinet, banjo, trombone and percussion.

At last all the elements came together, and we were able to start rehearsals on time. The countdown started and finally we had a show. Three talented puppeteers, Elizabeth Barron, Sarah Fitzpatrick and Soledad Zarate, worked extremely hard to bring the show to life with some wonderful feats of operating, as we persuaded the animals to

Molly with Mule and chickens

juggle, balance and tap dance to Stephen's music. The response was heart warming and exciting. "What you put in, you get out" is a wise adage, and all our efforts paid off.

Why is it that, during the creative process, one cannot imagine the rewards that will finally come?

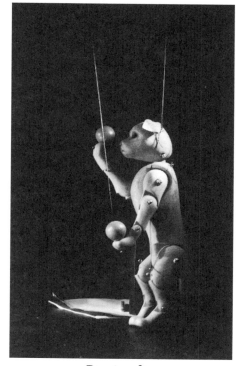

Dog juggling

Chapter 34

Oldies Don't Cry

> *The unexamined life is not worth living.*
> **Socrates** *(469–399 BC)*
> *in Plato's Apology*

It does not take long to start thinking about the next project – probably about a week! In mind now was a collection of poems introduced to us by a Capetonian publisher and friend, Gus Ferguson. Gus published a quarterly book of poetry in which appeared, occasionally, a piece by a poet named Finuala Dowling. And then a collection of hers was published entitled *Notes from the Dementia Ward*. This set us both thinking.

Despite the fact that we were both keen on the idea of making a production based on the poem, we flunked it. In the first instance we approached Howard Barker with the proposal that he might be willing to write a marionette play about dementia. He rejected such a project, asserting that the subject was far too fashionable.

It was difficult trying to produce a viable plan as to how one might present Dowling's poetry, let alone a subject like dementia. Her poems are never afraid of the truth, bitterly humorous and poignant. The breakthrough came during a visit to South Africa when Gren's sister Jill, and her husband David, took us on a most exotic weekend to Shingwedzi Rest Camp in a game park on the border with Mozambique. An annual event called Baroque in the Bush was taking place. The weekend was spent listening to divine classical music while, in the background, elephant were drinking at a waterhole. In between the musical interludes we attended lectures on baroque music given by the musical director. In one of the lessons we learned about slow and fast movements. This knowledge was to be crucial in the formation of our script. It was a breakthrough in how to present *Notes from the Dementia Ward*.

There is no particular discipline for the order of movements in musical compositions. We broke our script up into two parts, each with three movements, and then equated a fast movement to humour and a slow one to tragedy and used the poems accordingly. Our experience had taught us not to try and illustrate the poem because the poetry itself gives the listener images to think about. As the poem is spoken, the image on the stage remains still; this is followed by a visual metaphor, with movement and dialogue reflecting what the poem has conveyed to the audience.

One sequence illustrated a birthday celebration for an elderly patient at which a traditional Punch and Judy show took place.

A set of Punch and Judy figures, c. 1860

The Punch puppets were made to scale, as they were a show within the show. Glyn Edwards, renowned Punch expert and writer, was commissioned to write the Punch dialogue, using very traditional repartee between Punch and his wife Judy.

During the puppet-making period we arranged to attend a poetry festival at Snape Maltings in Suffolk, at which Ms Dowling was giving a reading. This was a real treat, as not only did we get to hear Finuala in person, but also she subsequently came to our home in Hackney and spent an evening with us during which we were able to talk about the production, show her the puppets and discuss the script.

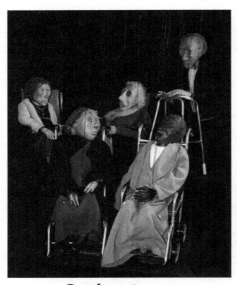
Care home inmates

In the writing, we made use of dialogue from an interview that Kate had conducted with a friend who had had the great misfortune to suffer from Alzheimer's. What he said reflected the essence of the piece and gave backbone to the dialogue sequences. As well as that recording, she had previously presented two short marionette pieces that conveyed different surreal aspects of human thought and behaviour. These two sequences became part of the production, which was now a fully qualified family affair as Stan painted the backdrops and Joshua, his brother, wrote the music. This was Josh's first full composition for Movingstage and included a beautiful trumpet solo for the end sequence, when a car is travelling along a mountain road.

The three-dimensional scenery was constructed by puppeteer and artist Juliette Meacock, while our friend and talented maker Colleen Magennis constructed wheelchairs, a Zimmer frame and a trolley on which our old lady heroine had an operation on her knee.

We made the show that we wanted, and not what we may have thought the audience would want. After much discussion, the title of the production was decided upon: *End Games*.

The audience did give us a positive response and that was enough for us to justify the huge effort involved in the making of the show. The experience taught us that when one is young, old age just does not exist, but as old age arrives one realises that it is not a pretty place, and that there is a very delicate balance between humour and tragedy.

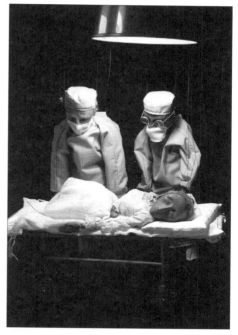

The operation

Isolation

Chapter 35

Portworthy

> *Money is like a sixth sense without which*
> *you cannot make a complete use of the other five.*
> W Somerset Maugham
> *Of Human Bondage (1915)*

Keeping up with the day-to-day business, publicity and bookings for the theatre is a big task. After years of managing this side of things, with some intermittent part-time help, we progressed to an online booking system and some wonderful part-time administration in the form of Soledad Zarate. Soledad had joined us as a trainee and then worked as a regular member of the team for several years. She is doubly skilled in that not only is she a great all-round puppeteer who can make and operate, but she is also very digitally clever. No problem on a computer is too tricky for her: social media, tweets, giant mailing lists by email, remote working – all are easily handled as part of a day's work.

By 2015, the gradual handover of the business was starting to take place as we slowed down and the family took on more responsibility. Juliet began to voice her concerns about the long-term condition of the barge and how long we could expect it to remain sound and "portworthy", as the saying goes.

Neither of us wanted the enterprise to become a burden in any way, particularly with regard to maintenance. The last time the barge had been out of the water in dry dock was around 2002, after the incident of the leak. Perish the thought that this might reoccur with the family in charge. Juliet began to consider how we might be able to finance a full survey of the hull and any work that would ensue as a result. It was then that Soledad came up with the idea of crowdfunding.

Gren inspects the barge on the hardstanding at Isleworth

The barge prior to going into the dry dock for refurbishment

We had been receiving emails from the crowdfunding platform Spacehive, encouraging us to put in an application to the Mayor of London's fund, and so we prepared a bid. We estimated that we required £21,000 to cover dry docking, a survey, repairs and renovations, new paintwork and signage. Soledad took on the whole project. She set it up online, preparing the site and the publicity that explained to the public what we needed, and out it went on the internet. The idea is that the more people who pledge money, the more popular your project appears and then, hopefully, the mayor's team see fit to put in the rest of the amount required. In our case we did not receive any funding from the mayor, but we decided to carry on and try to reach our target through crowdfunding for the total amount. Only if you reach the specified target do all the pledges get paid out. No money is received until that happens. The scheme began in May and our deadline was early October. Around mid-August things did not look good. We had about £13,000 worth of pledges and they had slowed down considerably since early summer. Soledad did everything she could, and we had a presentation day in the outside arena in Sheldon Square, next to the canal at Little Venice. Several of us operated trick puppets and handed out leaflets. Most people there were on their lunchbreaks and plugged into headphones or on laptops, not interested in what we were up to. Nothing was achieved; no pledges were forthcoming.

Soledad also set up a system of rewards for pledges, such as postcards, free tickets or, for £1000, a private performance. We made countless phone calls and sent out emails to people we knew and businesses we had worked with, including the dry dock. None of us enjoyed this kind of work; it is always hard asking for something and we had arguments as to who could pluck up enough nerve to approach certain firms or individuals!

In late September we had a trip booked to visit Gren's sister in South Africa. We flew to Johannesburg and then headed straight on to the Natal coast to Jill's place by the sea. We arrived some days before her and settled in for a break. When we left London, the total was around £17,000 and no one imagined that we could possibly reach the target in that last week. Although we had come for a holiday, the dreaded internet called us and, however hard we tried, we just had to keep checking the total on the site. The big problem was that the signal on the north Natal coast was very weak. We had to run down to the cliff edge, overlooking the sea, and wave our phones about, desperately looking for a signal. It became thrilling as the total rose.

Success! Amazement. People pledged big amounts, both anonymously and by name; some pledged a second time. We were quite overwhelmed with the interest and generosity that was apparent throughout, but extraordinary in the last three days. It seems that the excitement of actually reaching the target is catching, and for some marvellous and inexplicable reason people become even more generous in their desire to see us reach that goal. It was a great moment getting over the line and we felt huge relief and gratitude to all our supporters who made it possible for us to carry out the big overhaul.

Barge in the dry dock at last

The dry dock had been booked, optimistically, so when the season in Richmond finished, the barge team cruised downriver to Brentford and left the boat high and dry for the work to be done. All was carried out as planned – the survey was made and the plating, welding and patching done as needed. The hull was repainted under the water line and new anodes fitted. We returned to Little Venice in time for the autumn season and put on the winter tarpaulins. During the spring and summer months the barge is shaded by a set of awnings and these had become ragged and ripped. Having paid the boatyard for the work, there was still enough money to have a new set of awnings made and this we did. These were ready for summer 2017. We set up in Richmond looking smart and bright and knowing that all was well below the water line. Peace of mind descended, which made the continuing handover an easier process.

Voluntary labour, led by Amy Hazeldine, pulling the barge through the shallows

The handover had already begun, slowly rather than in a big dramatic ceremony, starting with us being able to hand over the moving of the barge between Little Venice and Richmond each summer. Rob and Stan now manage that and are able to draw on lots of voluntary labour to help. The annual journey to Richmond does have an element of fun for the crew.

At the start of 2017, Kate and Stan had mentioned a plan to make a Christmas production. Kate wrote the script, with input from Stanley, and then the making process began in earnest. By late spring all the characters had been cast, in terms of voices, and the recordings made. Stan was busy in the workshop carving and painting backdrops, and various other puppeteers were employed to make specific items. It was a new and interesting situation for both of us, watching a show being devised and designed, and decisions being made, without our involvement, as the thing developed. Juliet and Colleen were asked to make the shadow sequence and were pleased to be involved without having the ultimate responsibility of being in the driving seat! And so we watched it all take shape.

Stan Middleton sorts out the strings Photo by Paul Grover

As the production neared completion, with the scheduled opening looming ahead, we received a card from Kate which we, with her permission, reproduce here:

Dear Mum and Dad,

After much hair pulling and anxiety I think the rehearsals have got off to a good solid start! The puppets, lights and soundtrack are all lovely! Let's hope it all fits together like a glove!

I hope you're happy we're doing The Little Xmas Tree. I'm imagining that it must be strange and maybe hard not to be doing it yourself.

But I hope you feel that even if there are elements of the show that you don't like, or wouldn't have done like us, you feel it's professional and true to you, Movingstage and the legacy of the barge. This is very important to me.

I'm looking forward to it all being over! But hopefully we will end up with a new, fun, thoughtful show for the repertoire.

Love

Kate

Needless to say, receiving such a sensitive card was wonderful. Knowing that Kate is aware of our oldie sensibilities is a help towards facing up to the ultimate submission that will have to be accepted in the end!

The summer 2017 tour to Richmond, with evening performances of *The River Girl*, required much time and attention. When we returned to Little Venice in the autumn, we ran a short season of ten performances and were delighted when Wendy Cope came to one of them. She gave us a warm thumbs-up saying she had forgotten what she had written! She seemed genuinely happy with the play, which is without doubt still relevant, especially now when gender politics is top of the agenda.

The new play was launched for Christmas in Little Venice, with immense hard work and input from the production team for the last push. The bookings were excellent and after the flurry of the first few days, it became clear that the audiences were more than happy. Feedback filtered through and, as the play settled down, we realised slowly but surely that it was working well and that it was a real success.

This new Christmas production included many characters and a magical plot line that can be enjoyed by children and adults alike:

Xmas Tree Man: The time has come to plant this seed. I've no idea if it'll grow as it's been sitting in my desk for years. But my grandmother said to me, that it was like a precious little stone and when I needed some help I should plant it. Well I need a bit of help now.

Most of these marionettes had been in previous productions, and having passed the strict audition procedure, managed to get a part in the play. They were re-dressed as their new characters and took on their new roles.

The Little Christmas Tree cast – Rat was fired and lost the part

Chapter 36

Posterity

Perfect freedom is reserved for the man
who lives by his own work and in that
work does what he wants to do.
R G Collingwood
Speculum Mentis (1924)

Slowly but surely one must accept that all good things come to an end, including the ability to make shows and the freedom that goes with it. In this regard, it is extremely lucky if there is a family trained up to take over, and if they *want* to take over. Given those two criteria one must be prepared to hand over authority and leave decision making to others. If this can be accepted, then a period of luxury will follow.

We are very fortunate and privileged that our family live in the same borough as us, are interested in taking over the Puppet Barge and in keeping the show on the "road". The process is not a quick, easy bit of surgery but a more drawn-out affair. Various influences are continually in force, including the imparting of knowledge acquired over a very long period.

Puppetry art is honed, not only by teaching, but also by observation and the practice of operating in a show. We have trained a number of people over the past decades, approximately two young people each year for 35 years, and out of the seventy-odd potential marionettists we reckon about fifteen have stayed the course – a success rate of around 22 percent. We consider this to be highly successful. Not only do we have trained, professional marionettists to work with, but we can also boast a host of wonderful friends.

The process of training is not difficult if the trainee is keen and willing to work hard for not much reward other than what the job offers. As Eleanor Roosevelt once said: *"One's philosophy is not best expressed in words; it's expressed in the choices one makes. In the long run, we shape our lives and we shape ourselves. The process never ends until we die. And the choices we make are ultimately our responsibility."*

There is a special award for marionettists, created by Eric Bramall who set up the Harlequin Puppet Theatre in Wales. The Harlequin was the first marionette theatre in the UK to be designed by architects Ove Arup and built

Picture postcard – subject unknown

from scratch. We won this award in the year 2000. Seventeen years later, Stan and Soledad Zarate, his partner in String Theatre, won it for *The Red Balloon* and *The Insect Circus*, their two very successful productions.

Stan Middleton started his training at two years old. Grenville began his theatre experience at the age of seven, raising money for the war effort. Kate started in her early teens and Juliet joined the Little Angel to begin her puppet career aged 32. Additional family members have contributed their skills: Louise Middleton, a trained actress, has provided many excellent voiceovers; Natasha Middleton has operated on many shows and led school workshops; Joshua Middleton is a composer and sound editor. Rob supplies technical, nautical and directorial skills in equal measure, all of which underpin daily activities and are essential in keeping us afloat. We are all waiting to see Tom prove himself. He is currently good at brass polishing, and this keeps the barge smart.

There is a story about a man who inherited his father's old axe, a cherished item. He continued to use it as both his grandfather and his

The old and new management: Juliet, Stanley, Grenville, Katherine, Robert

father had used it. After a year or two he had to renew the handle and then a few years later he had to renew the axe head as well. He, of course, continued to think that he was still using his grandfather's axe, when in fact he was using a new one! No doubt the same could happen to the barge.

As it happens, the barge has already had a new bottom overlaid on top of the old one, as well as some plating on the sides; it is possible that over the years it will become an entirely different vessel from the one that we found on the beach, in the old yard on the Thames.

Although the next generations will not have the problem of starting from scratch, as their inheritance will be fairly significant, they already know that money is not easy and can disappear into the wind without one realising it.

Puppet theatre is unique within the world of entertainment and cannot be compared with the actor's theatre, ballet or musical theatre. Its nearest cousin is possibly opera. One great advantage of the puppet business is that the marionettist does not have to manage actors. Puppets are an easier breed. The main disadvantage is that there is less money available for the puppet business, probably because of prejudice and the freedom of thought and action that puppeteers display.

The marionettist does not have to manage actors

The "marionette proprietor" carries artistic and financial responsibility for the puppets, the shows and all aspects of the company. It is possible to share these proprietorial tasks. In the case of running a theatre on a vessel, the skills required are various and very different, including navigational ability and knowledge of the water, be it canal or river. Puppet theatre on a barge cannot be compared with any other theatrical facility or entertainment.

The new generation has discovered freedom, but now it has to take note of what Joseph Stiglitz says on the subject: "The essence of freedom is the right to make a choice – and to accept the responsibility that comes with it".

Having acquired our own freedom over the years, it will, of course, eventually come to an end, and the process of losing it is inevitably painful. It is a great privilege to be able to hand the baton on to one's own family so that the freedom will endure. It becomes a case of "absolute submission".

Stone work in a Swedish country arts centre – a former stately home

So, the handover feels almost complete. The next generation has risen to the challenge and written and produced new work for the barge. This has played to full houses and is a proven success that will remain in the repertoire for years to come.

Now the barge theatre can move forward through the next decades with confidence and creative ability at the helm. Things will change, be done differently, move into a new age and speak with another voice; all of which is right. Nothing stands still unless it stagnates. It is a new era and the new company will make those changes to coincide with their own artistic vision. We wish them well and feel proud and grateful that they have chosen this route. May it be as exciting, surprising, engrossing and rewarding as it was for us.

Appendix 1

**(i) The following is the first paragraph in Chapter One of
John Wright's book, Your Puppetry**

*"Most things made in our time are evolved from plans or drawings. Take, for
instance, those complicated masses of lines and letters which enable architects
and engineers to set down their first ideas, and to develop from them a final
scheme. They represent as a rule half or more of the total creative task under
taken. It would be wrong to suggest such detailed, accurate and complex
drawings as the average architectural work, but there is no doubt that some
form of design, however elementary, will be of enormous help in the evolution
of your first puppet. As you progress, you will find that your ability as a designer
and draughtsman will improve steadily with every figure you produce."*

**(ii) The following note appears in:
Ionesco's book, Notes & Counter Notes**

*"Another kind of drama is still possible. More powerful and far richer.
Drama that is not symbolist, but symbolic; not allegorical, but mythical;
that springs from our everlasting anguish; drama where the invisible become
visible, where ideas are translated into concrete images, of reality, where the
problem is expressed in flesh and blood; where anguish is a living presence,
an impressive witness; drama that might puzzle the sociologists but could
stimulate and quicken all that is un- scientific in the scientist; and, reaching
beyond his ignorance, the common man."*

**(iii) The following sentence appears in: George Speaight's, *History
of the English Puppet Theatre***

*"Our imagination will give life to the inscrutable countenance of the
marionette."*

(iv) The following quote is from a transcript from a John Phillips Memorial Lecture delivered at the Theatre Museum, London 8 March 2003 edited by Poh Sim Plowright

In all the theories of acting promulgated in the West the last hundred years whether from Stanislavsky or Brecht or Kleist or Craig, the central debate has been about how far the actor inhabits or presents the role he or she is playing. And across the board in East and West , it has been realized that the greatest stumbling-block to a successful performance is the ego. It is not surprising that Zeami (one of the founders of Noh) chose the ego-less string puppet as his model when teaching his actors how to move. Let me quote you his famous admonition to his disciples:

"Turn yourself into a puppet made of wood; it has no ego, it thinks nothing; and let the body and limbs work themselves out in accordance with the discipline they have undergone this is the way to win."

Appendix 2

Excerpt from the Theatres Act 1968

" play " means—

    (*a*) any dramatic piece, whether involving improvisation or not, which is given wholly or in part by one or more persons actually present and performing and in which the whole or a major proportion of what is done by the person or persons performing, whether by way of speech, singing or action, involves the playing of a role ; and

    (*b*) any ballet given wholly or in part by one or more persons actually present and performing, whether or not it falls within paragraph (*a*) of this definition ;

" police officer " means a member, or in Scotland a constable, of a police force ;

" premises " includes any place ;

"public performance" includes any performance in a public place within the meaning of the Public Order Act 1936 and any performance which the public or any section thereof are permitted to attend, whether on payment or otherwise ;

" script " has the meaning assigned by section 9(2) of this Act.

Appendix 3

No Objection Certificate issued in Karachi – 1982

OFFICE OF THE DEPUTY COMMISSIONER & D.M. SOUTH, KARACHI

NO. D.C. (S)/NOC/ *179* /198 , Karachi, the *25.2.82*

NO OBJECTION CERTIFICATE

There is no objection to the holding of Puppet Show (Bottom's Dream money Business,the Birdman in english) by Mr. Faizaan Peerada, M.D. of Rafi Peer Theatre Workshop, Karachi inside Y.M.C.A. ground.
on from to

subject to the availability of premises and clearence from Excise & Taxation Department, Karachi and on the condition that no obstruction and disturbance is caused to the general public and traffic. Display of female and dancing and game of chance, raffle, tambola or any type of gambling not allowed. THE PROVISIONS OF LOUD SPEAKER ORDINANCE AND MLRs/MLOs SHOULD STRICTLY BE FOLLOWED.

For DEPUTY COMMISSIONER & D.M.
SOUTH, KARACHI.

Copy to :-

1. The S.P. Civil Lines 2. S.D.M. Civil Lines

3. The Director E & T. 4. The SHO A/Maidan 5. The applicant.

Appendix 4

10 Videos on UTube
Puppet Barge Trailer
Strings
End Games
Red Riding Hood
Brer Rabbit Trailer
Time Trip Puppets used in Horizon documentary for BBC
Dreams on the River Parts 1,2 & 3
What's On
The Pig Attraction An episode from the TV series
London Calling

https://www.youtube.com/user/ThePuppetBarge?feature=mhum+-+p%2Fa%2Fu%2F0%2FkEd9HiBtpKI

Cultural Camera
https://www.youtube.com/watch?v=Lqxxd4BS5D0

Get Reel - Video Film Workshop
http://www.youtube.com/watch?v=yIMCuKZ-2uA

Puppet Theatre Barge commercial
http://www.youtube.com/watch?v=S590i_1hlAs

Barging In
https://www.youtube.com/watch?v=kEd9HiBtpKI

Richmond
https://www.youtube.com/watch?v=k4xTOlnhFnY

Puppet Theatre working on Newsnight in the 1990's
https://www.youtube.com/watch?v=CPs4ABIyXwY

Appendix 5

A Dedication to John Wright as read by Gren Middleton at his memorial

"It has been my privilege to have spent the last fifteen years sparring with a champion gaining formidable experience and knowledge and I believe everyone here will have learnt something from John. Here is a poem, the words of a Zulu miner's song, to send him on his way."

Song of the Mine Worker

Come let us be going my brother
Let's make for home.
Come, let us be off to see the small hills of Tugela.
We worked too long there, down the mines
an age ago we left our homes
 for this place, this Gold-town.
When we come home they will be waiting
mothers rejoicing as we cross the step
to home, home, my home.
Come brother, let's make for home.
Oh return, leave the Gold-town
leave the uses of the city
caress our children
love our father's people
and they'll speak then with hand clappings
and happiness as we go in
they'll be waiting there at home.
Come, come home.

This poem was printed in the Penguin Book of South African verse, after it was read the editor of the book declared himself to Gren. He was Jack Cope an old friend of John Wright's and a well known South African poet, who was also at the ceremony.

Appendix 6

The Puppet Barge
A villanelle

It is time to move the Puppet Barge,
The tides and winds both play a part.
And on we go for this is life, a wild mirage.

Ferryman knows the rules, writ large.
He sings out loud as he loads his cart.
It is time to move the Puppet Barge.

The rowing boats towards us charge.
Give way to port! The skipper shouts.
And on we go for this is life, a wild mirage.

Check water, oil and battery charge.
The skipper shouts the orders brief,
It is time to move the Puppet Barge.

The engineer leaves the garage.
The engine screams, the night arrives.
And on we go for this is life, a wild mirage.

The lights shine bright, it's like the Taj.
We really want to be in bed.
It is time to move the Puppet Barge.
And on we go, for this is life a wild mirage.

GM

Appendix 7

THE LONDON-MUNICH PUPPET PLAYERS

George Speaight - Susanne Forster - Stefan Fichert

6 Maze Road
Kew Gardens
Richmond
Surrey TW9 3DA
01 940 3757

Jägerstrasse 1
D 8035
Gauting
    bei München
(010 4989) 850 1364

24 May 1985

Dear Gren

    The Port of London Authority has now given
us permission to moor the Puppet Theatre Barge at
Richmond between September 3 and 8. Bamber Gascoigne
is willing to provide electric power from his boat house
on the riverside. Could we have an early meeting to
survey the site and discuss the various problems that
will arise?

    These include: how to carry the electric cable
from the boat house to the barge; how to cope with the
shallow water at low tide (between 2 ft and 4 ft); the
PLA say we would need to lie some 8 ft from the river
wall; have you a sufficiently long gang plank? Also the
area is liable to flooding at high tide; I have a table
of the days and hours when high water may be expected.
The grass verge may be muddy, and planks will be needed
to enable patrons to cross it.

    So there will be much to discuss, including
just how we shall moor. The grass verge is only
down stream, and there are no bollards.

    I await your call before you get too involved in
your own hazardous voyage.

    Anyhow, whatever problems come up, this is good
news.

        Love,
        George

Appendix 8

The Barge 'If' for Puppeteers

If you can dress to make yourself attractive,
Yet not make puffs and curls your chief delight,
If you can swim and row, be strong and active,
    But of the gentler graces lose not sight:

If you can dance without a craze for dancing,
    Play without giving play too strong a hold,
Enjoy the love of friends without romancing,
    Care for the weak the friendless and the old:

If you can master brass work and tarpaulin
    And not acquire, as well, a priggish mien
If you can feel the touch of silk and satin
    Without despising calico and jean

If you can use a chisel and a hammer –
Can do both man and women's work, when need occurs;
Can sing, when asked, without excuse and stammer.
    And rise above unfriendly smiles and slurs:

If you can make good bread as well as curries.
    Can sew with skill and have an eye for dust;
If you can be a friend and hold no worries,
You'll be one all will love – because they must:

If sometime you should meet and love another
    And make a space of much tranquillity
If you can be both father and a mother.
    You'll be a person of ability

The plan that's been developed through the ages,
And win the best that life can have in store-
You'll be my friend, a model for the sages.
A puppeteer whom all will bow before.

After Kipling

Appendix 9

Plans of the Puppet Theatre Barge
by Arijit Chatterjee and Asha Sumra

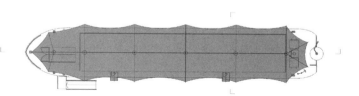

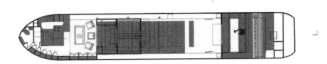

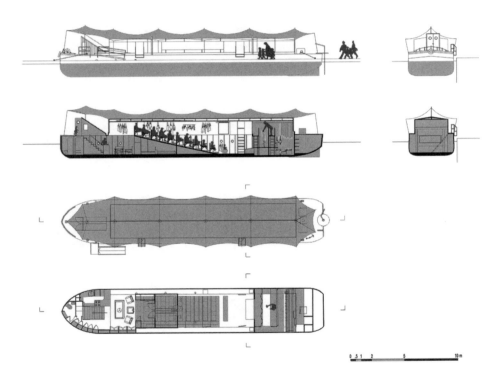

Index

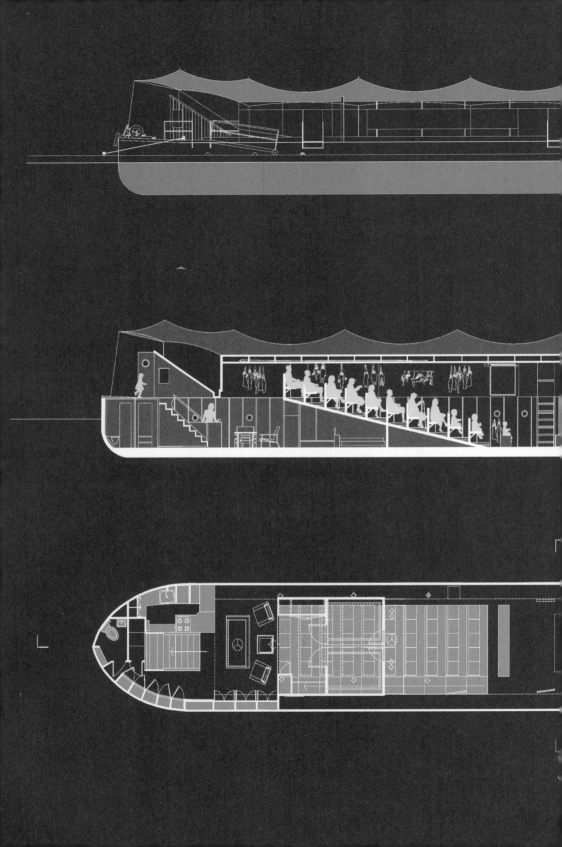